Microservices, IoT, and Azure

Leveraging DevOps and
Microservice Architecture
to Deliver SaaS Solutions

Bob Familiar

Apress®

Microservices, IoT, and Azure: Leveraging DevOps and Microservice Architecture to Deliver SaaS Solutions

ISBN-13 (pbk): 978-1-4842-1276-9

ISBN-13 (electronic): 978-1-4842-1275-2

Managing Director: Welmoed Spahr
Lead Editor: James DeWolf
Development Editor: Douglas Pundick
Technical Reviewer: Jeff Barnes
Editorial Board: Steve Anglin, Gary Cornell, Louise Corrigan, James T. DeWolf,
    Jonathan Gennick, Robert Hutchinson, Michelle Lowman, James Markham,
    Susan McDermott, Matthew Moodie, Jeffrey Pepper, Douglas Pundick, Ben Renow-Clarke,
    Gwenan Spearing, Matt Wade, Steve Weiss
Coordinating Editor: Melissa Maldonado
Copy Editor: Mary Behr
Compositor: SPi Global
Indexer: SPi Global
Artist: SPi Global

Distributed to the book trade worldwide by Springer Science+Business Media New York, 233 Spring Street, 6th Floor, New York, NY 10013. Phone 1-800-SPRINGER, fax (201) 348-4505, e-mail orders-ny@springer-sbm.com, or visit www.springer.com. Apress Media, LLC is a California LLC and the sole member (owner) is Springer Science + Business Media Finance Inc. (SSBM Finance Inc.). SSBM Finance Inc. is a Delaware corporation.

For information on translations, please e-mail rights@apress.com, or visit www.apress.com.

Apress and friends of ED books may be purchased in bulk for academic, corporate, or promotional use. eBook versions and licenses are also available for most titles. For more information, reference our Special Bulk Sales–eBook Licensing web page at www.apress.com/bulk-sales.

Any source code or other supplementary materials referenced by the author in this text is available to readers at www.apress.com. For detailed information about how to locate your book's source code, go to www.apress.com/source-code/.

I dedicate this book to my incredible wife, Mandy, who is a continuous stream of inspiration and to my children, Ariana and Bobby, who never cease to amaze me with their talent, insight, and intelligence.

Contents at a Glance

Contents

About the Author

Bob Familiar is the Practice Director for Cloud & Services at BlueMetal. BlueMetal is a Modern Application company and the Cloud & Services team is a practitioner of lean engineering, a high velocity product development process that applies lean methodology, service-oriented patterns and practices, automation, and cloud platform capabilities for the design and development of modern applications.

Bob Familiar has been in the software industry for 30 years, having worked for both ISVs such as Dunn & Bradstreet Software and ON Technology and for Microsoft as a Principal Consultant, Architect Evangelist, and Director of Technology Evangelism. Bob holds a Masters in Computer Science from Northeastern and a patent for Object Relational Database and Distributed Computing.

About the Technical Reviewer

Jeff A. Barnes is a Cloud Solution Architect (CSA) on the Microsoft Partner Enterprise Architecture Team (PEAT), where he engages with leading cloud architects to present Microsoft's cloud vision. A 17+ year Microsoft veteran, Jeff brings over 30 years of deep technical experience to the CSA role. He typically works with key ISVs and global partners to demonstrate how Microsoft Azure technologies can be best leveraged to meet the current and future demands of an organization transitioning to the cloud. Jeff has deep practical experience in the retail, financial, and manufacturing industries and is a frequent speaker at Microsoft and third-party events. Jeff resides in Miami, Florida with his family, where his definition of "offshore development" usually equates to "fishing offshore."

Acknowledgments

I would like to thank Liam Spaeth, who has dedicated his life to both inspiring me with his creativity and keeping me employed for the past 20 years, and the leadership team at BlueMetal, Scott Jamison and Matt Jackson, for their support and encouragement.

A big thank you to my dear friend Jeff Barnes for his technical expertise and guidance throughout the process and to Vaclav Turecek and Mike Fussell from the Azure Service Fabric team for their input.

I would like to thank David McIntyre for his contribution to the sample code base, the Home Biomedical Dashboard.

Finally, I would like to thank Ron Bokleman, my PowerShell Sensei, who was instrumental in the creation of the automation scripts for the reference implementation.

Introduction

Microservices, IoT, and Azure make the case for adopting a high velocity, continuous delivery process to create reliable, scalable Software as a Service solutions that are designed and built using a microservice architecture, deployed to the Azure cloud, and managed through automation. SaaS applications are software products that are available 24x7, work on any device, scale elastically, and are resilient to change. This book provides software developers, architects, and operations engineers with practical guidance on this approach to software development through code, script, exercises, and a working reference implementation.

A working definition of microservices will be presented, and the approach will be contrasted with traditional, monolithic, layered architecture. A reference implementation for a fictitious home-biomedical startup will be used to demonstrate microservice architecture and automation capabilities for cross-cutting and business services as well as connected device scenarios for Internet of Things (IoT). Several Azure PaaS services will be detailed including storage, SQL Database, DocumentDb, Redis Cache, Cloud Services, Web APIs, API management, IoT Hub, IoT Suite, Event Hub, Stream Analytics. Finally, we will look to the future and examine Service Fabric to see how microservices are becoming the de facto approach to building reliable software in the cloud.

The Reference Implementation

The Reference Implementation provides automation scripts and source code for several microservices along with several client applications that play various roles in the context of the solution. The PowerShell scripts automate the provisioning, build, and deployment tasks that get the Home Biomedical solution up and running in Azure. In order to control costs of running the reference implementation, deprovisioning scripts are also provided.

The reference implementation consists of several independent microservices built using C#, ASP.NET Web API, DocumentDb, and Redis Cache and deployed as Azure websites. In addition, there is an IoT subsystem that is built using Event Hub, Stream Analytics, Cloud Services, and SQL Database. There is a sample real-time data visualization client that demonstrates how to orchestrate the microservices into a complete solution.

Viewed as a whole, the Reference Implementation demonstrates how to use several Azure PaaS services along with custom code and automation scripts to create a complete, modern application.

You will learn…

The combination of the book and the reference implementation provide a resource to learn the following:

- What microservices are and why they are a compelling architecture pattern for SaaS applications

- How to design, develop, and deploy microservices using Visual Studio, PowerShell, and Azure

- Microservice patterns for cross-cutting concerns and business capabilities

- Microservice patterns for Internet of Things and big data analytics solutions using IoT Hub, Event Hub, and Stream Analytics

- Techniques for automating microservice provisioning, build, and deployment

- What Service Fabric is and why it is the future direction for microservices on Microsoft Azure

Chapter 1: From Monolithic to Microservice - Shifting demographics and competitive pressure on business to drive impact at velocity is requiring us to evolve our approach to how we develop, deploy, and support our software products. This chapter lays out a roadmap to evolve not only application architecture but also process and organization.

Chapter 2: What Is a Microservice? - This chapter provides a working definition of microservices and details the benefits as well as the challenges to evolving to this architecture pattern.

Chapter 3: Microservice Architecture - Traditionally, we have used separation of concerns, a design principle for separating implementation into distinct layers in order to define horizontal seams in our application architecture. Microservice architecture applies separation of concern to identify vertical seams that define their isolation and autonomous nature. This chapter will compare and contrast microservice architecture with traditional layered architecture.

Chapter 4: Azure – A Microservice Platform - The Azure platform exudes characteristics of microservices. This chapter examines several Azure services to identify common patterns of services that are designed and implemented using microservices. Storage, SQL Database, DocumentDb, Redis Cache, Service Bus, API management, and app containers are reviewed.

Chapter 5: Automation - Automation is the key to being able to evolve to a continuous delivery approach and realize the benefits of SaaS. This chapter outlines a framework for defining and organizing your automation process and takes you through 10 exercises that will provision, build, and deploy the reference implementation using PowerShell.

Chapter 6: Microservice Reference Implementation - The epic story of Home Biomedical, a wholly owned subsidiary of LooksFamiliar, Inc., is detailed, and the implementation details of the reference microservices are revealed. The common libraries for ReST calls and DocumentDb and Redis Cache for data access are reviewed. Designing for both public and management APIs is discussed along with the implementation details for the model, interface, service, API, SDK, and console components.

Chapter 7: IoT and Microservices - IoT is becoming a more common solution pattern as we learn to incorporate streaming data into our solutions. This chapter outlines the capabilities needed to realize an IoT solution and maps them to the Azure IoT stack. IoT Hub, IoT Suite, Event Hub, and Stream Analytics are detailed, as is how to use Event Hub, Cloud Services, and Notification Hub to support mobile alerts. A working example of data visualization using a JavaScript client along with SignalR, ReST, and SQL Database is reviewed.

Chapter 8: Service Fabric - Service Fabric is the microservice management, runtime, and infrastructure that Microsoft uses to build, deploy, and manage their own first-class cloud services such as SQL Database, DocumentDb, Bing Cortana, Halo Online, Skype for Business, In Tune, Event Hubs, and many others. This chapter provides a primer and demonstrates Service Fabric by migrating one of the Web API microservices to Service Fabric.

CHAPTER 1

■ ■ ■

From Monolithic to Microservice

The days of paper-based transactions have passed and the days of small-scale web solutions for Intranet or online customer interaction are nearly forgotten. The monolithic software systems that were designed to function in those worlds are now struggling to keep pace with the expectations of both customers and the business. It is now imperative for companies to provide a modern digital experience for their customers and a platform for the business that can be used to drive impact and derive insight at velocity.

In order to meet the demands of a modern customer base, all companies, regardless of their stated business, must come to the realization that they are also in the software business. That may not be their primary persona but it has become the primary way that their customers expect to interact with them. Demographics are continually shifting, and the expectation of these new customers is that they will engage the companies they choose to do business with digitally. They expect that the experience is beautiful, feature-rich, and fast. They also expect that the experience is reachable and fully functional 24 hours a day, 7 days a week from any device.

It has fallen to us as the software developers, architects, and operations engineers to deliver new, scalable solutions that meet the expectations of customers and the business. We are being asked to deliver more features and functions and to do it with less: less time, less resources. And if you are like most software professionals, you are also responsible for a portfolio of aging, legacy systems that house the ever important business logic somewhere within impenetrable brambles of code and data.

There does exist a software product model that both meets the expectations of customers and provides a platform to drive business outcomes at velocity. That model is called Software as a Service (SaaS). Let's examine the characteristics of a SaaS solution to see how it may provide a means by which we can extricate ourselves from the thorns, spines, and prickles of monolithic legacy applications.

Software as a Service

The Software as a Service model implies that your software product is available 24/7, scales elastically, is highly available and fault tolerant, provides a responsive user experience on all popular devices, and does not require the user to install a client or perform updates or patches. The software product is always the most recent and up-to-date version and is deployed and maintained using a process called Continuous Delivery.

Continuous Delivery

The Continuous Delivery process is defined by the following capabilities:

- The software is developed in a high-velocity, iterative approach and is deployable throughout its lifecycle.

- Deployment to dev, test, staging, and production is managed using an on-demand automated process.

- If there is ever any issue with the deployment process, fixing it takes higher priority over delivering new features.

Continuous Delivery requires a product-oriented software development process that is guided by a set of unwavering principles that prioritizes the frequent release of high-quality working software.

Agile and Scrum

Agile and Scrum have become the prevalent methodology and process for high-velocity software development with teams organized into small cross-functional groups and whose goal is to deliver working, running software at the close of every sprint. Agile defines a set of core principles that are known as the Agile Manifesto:

- We value individuals and interactions over processes and tools.

- We value working software over comprehensive documentation.

- We value customer collaboration over contract negotiation.

- We value responding to change over following a plan.

- That is, while there is value in the items on the right, we value the items on the left more.

In order to apply these principles in the context of an actual project, Ken Schwaber and Jeff Sutherland introduced Scrum, an evolutionary, adaptive, and self-correcting approach to the software development process. Scrum is lightweight, simple to understand, but difficult to master. As with any endeavor, discipline is required in order to achieve a high-quality result.

Scrum is based on an empirical process control theory that asserts that knowledge comes from experience and decisions should be based on what is known. Scrum uses an iterative, incremental approach in order to forecast and reduce risk.

There are three pillars to the Scrum Process:

- **Transparency**: A common language is used to describe the process and is used by all members of the team.

- **Inspection**: Scrum artifacts are frequently inspected in order to detect variances in progress toward a goal.

- **Adaptation**: If it is determined that an aspect of the process will produce an undesirable outcome, the process must be adjusted as soon as possible to minimize damage.

The Scrum Team works together through the well-defined Scrum Process to develop a product backlog, identifying a set of backlog items that will be developed during a two- to four-week sprint called the Sprint Backlog. The Scrum Master and Development Team meet daily in the Daily Scrum to identify what was accomplished the previous day, what will be done today, and if there are any blocking items. This process is monitored closely to determine if the sprint is on track or not. At the close of the sprint, running software is delivered and a Sprint Retrospective meeting is held to review progress and provide input into the next phase of sprint planning.

Scrum, when combined with Agile Principles, provides a process that is more in harmony with the way that software developers work individually and as teams, and has resulted in increased velocity and quality over the traditional gated waterfall process. Software development techniques have emerged from this new way of teaming, such as the use of immutable interfaces and mock objects to support independent workstreams and early testing.

In addition to the need for a high-velocity, high-quality development process, Software as a Service requires a set of principles and processes related to bringing software products to market. Lean engineering is a methodology and process that looks to increase product quality and customer satisfaction by including the customer in the process and providing access to the product early and often. Customers can provide critical feedback that is used to guide product design.

Lean Engineering

Lean engineering has risen out of the startup space and defines a high-velocity product development approach that builds on Agile and Scrum to include deployment into production so as to gather telemetry from the product as well as from the customers using the product. This learning is then folded into the next development iteration (see Figure 1-1).

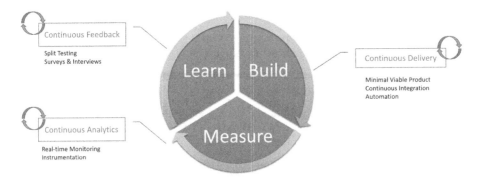

Figure 1-1. *Lean engineering's Build-Measure-Learn cycle*

The Lean engineering cycle is called Build-Measure-Learn and promotes Continuous Delivery, Continuous Analytics, and Continuous Feedback. The creation of dashboards, either developed or provided by third-party tools, are instituted to provide the real-time and historical analytics from which you can derive insights quickly and steer the product development effort in the direction that meets your customer's needs.

DevOps

In order to support a Lean Engineering, Continuous Delivery product development lifecycle, you must automate the development process, called DevOps. DevOps is both a culture and a set of technologies and tools used for automation.

The cultural aspect of DevOps can be the most challenging to organizations. DevOps implies the reorganization of teams combining developers, architects, and quality assurance together with operations. It also requires the adoption of new methodologies, processes, platforms, and tools. It is something that does not happen overnight and should be approached in a phased manner using small teams that adopt the new methods and then transition to become subject matter experts, transferring their knowledge to the rest of the staff.

Cloud

SaaS solutions require an infrastructure and software platform that can provide high availability, fault tolerance, elastic scale, and on-demand storage and compute. In other words, SaaS is a software model designed for the cloud. Cloud platforms such as Amazon's AWS and Microsoft's Azure are themselves Software as a Service platforms that provide all the building blocks needed for the creation of SaaS solutions.

Cloud computing introduced the concept of a managed virtual environment that offers levels of choice with respect to how much of the platform you want to be responsible for maintaining. The terms Infrastructure as a Service (IaaS), Platform as a Service (PaaS), and Software as a Service (SaaS) were introduced to define these choices (see Figure 1-2).

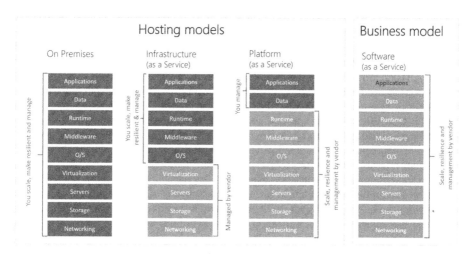

Figure 1-2. *Cloud Hosting Models*

- **Infrastructure as a Service:** A cloud provider offers the network, virtual machines, and storage on demand. Users of this model are responsible for all the layers above the VM level including OS configuration and patching.

- **Platform as a Service:** A cloud provider offers to maintain the operating system, provide middleware such as databases, enterprise messaging, and runtime containers for application code. Users of this model can focus on the capabilities of their application and automating deployment.

- **Software as a Service:** A business model where the entire software and hardware stack of a solution is managed by the cloud provider and often offered through a subscription model.

Cloud platforms are feature-rich, technically sophisticated platforms that provide a wide expanse of capability that can be provisioned on demand and in many locations around the globe, providing a global footprint for your solutions if necessary. At a high level, cloud platforms provide infrastructure, storage, compute, and application services on demand through automation via ReST APIs and a pay-as-you-go model (where you only pay for what you use). The ability to support a high-velocity product lifecycle that moves a software product through a dev, test, stage, and production environment is now possible without making huge investments in on-premises infrastructure.

In the past, when we designed software for a specific platform, there were best practices and architecture patterns that were optimal for that platform. You would typically map your software architecture to the underlying architecture in order to be compliant and take full advantage of system services. Cloud platforms are no different. The underlying architecture of cloud platforms is called microservice architecture. As you look to adopt cloud platforms for your solution, the recommended architecture pattern is microservice architecture. Using this architecture pattern you can take full advantage of underlying services that cloud platforms provide.

Microservices

A microservice is a software building block that does one thing and does it well. It can be provisioned on demand, elastically scaled, provides fault tolerance and fail over, and when it is no longer needed can be de-provisioned. All the capabilities provided by commercial cloud platforms are themselves microservices that can be automated through scripting languages providing the on-demand control that DevOps requires.

When designing your own Software as a Service solution, the recommended platform is the cloud and the recommended architecture is microservices. Each business capability of your solution is designed, developed, tested, and deployed as an isolated, autonomous microservice that receives its elastic scale, fault tolerance, and automation from the cloud platform. Each business capability is separate and distinct from the others and can be maintained and enhanced without impacting any other part of the system. This provides the business the platform it needs to deliver enhancements, updates, and new features at velocity, without impacting the stability of the system.

With both client/server and n-tier architectures, we have been slicing our architectures horizontally in order to take advantage of the advancements in hardware during those eras and distributing the layers of code across ever larger server farms. We have been providing communication between these layers using a service-oriented, loosely coupled approach (see Figure 1-3).

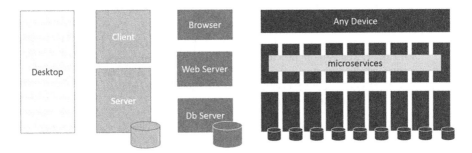

Figure 1-3. *Architecture by the slice*

These were the right decisions for their time, but as we move into the era of the cloud, we want to take advantage of the automation, elasticity, and resilience of the IaaS and PaaS features of cloud platforms. The approach of distributing monolithic blocks of code across server instances, while still viable in the cloud, is not the best approach to take advantage of the on-demand and elastic scale nature of cloud platforms. It prevents us from being able to provide the high-velocity, reliable releases required by new business models. Monolithic product releases are slowed down as small changes cause full system builds and test cycles.

Summary

In this chapter, you learned that in order to meet the expectations of customers and provide the business with a platform for driving impact at velocity, a new approach is required in the design, development, and deployment of our software products. The desired model is Software as a Service which implies the application of Continuous Delivery, Automation through DevOps, adoption of an automatable, scalable, elastic, highly resilient cloud platform and a microservice architecture.

Next we will define microservice architecture and learn how it contrasts with traditional monolithic layered architecture. You will learn how Microsoft Azure provides foundational services for storage, compute, messaging, telemetry, and much more, and you will learn how to leverage those services in the creation of your own microservice catalog. You will use a reference implementation that demonstrates these capabilities for both traditional applications as well as connected device scenarios for Internet of Things. Finally, you will look to the future, to where Azure is headed, to see how microservices are becoming the de facto approach to building in the cloud.

CHAPTER 2

■ ■ ■

What Is a Microservice?

Architecture is a result of a process of asking questions and testing them and re-interrogating and changing in a repetitive way.

—Thom Mayne

Software as a Service has emerged as a model for modern software products that provide customers a great experience and the business a dynamic platform for campaigns, communication, and the release of new features at a frequent pace. You learned in the last chapter that Agile and Scrum, Lean Engineering, and DevOps provide a methodology and process framework for high-velocity product development. You learned that cloud platforms provide an excellent foundation for SaaS solutions with their on-demand infrastructure and application services. Finally, you identified microservice architecture as the optimal architecture for cloud-hosted solutions. In this chapter, we will define microservices and discuss both the benefits and the challenges of this new approach.

Microservices Are...

The term *microservice* can be a bit misleading. The prefix "micro" implies that microservices are either tiny little entities that run around doing tasks on our behalf, like vacuuming the floor or fixing a flat tire, or that form a vast swarm of microscopic insect-like devices that self-replicate through the consumption of matter and energy, and are capable of disintegrating any substance they touch. Microservices do work on our behalf but they are not always tiny.

The "micro" in microservices is actually in reference to the scope of functionality that the service provides. A microservice provides a business or platform capability through a well-defined API, data contract, and configuration. It provides this function and only this function. It does one thing and it does it well. This simple concept provides the foundation for a framework that will guide the design, development, and deployment of your microservices.

Within the context of doing one thing and doing it well, microservices also exhibit a number of other properties and behaviors; it is these elements that differentiate microservices from previous incarnations of service-oriented approaches. These elements affect every aspect of how we develop software today, from team structure, source code organization, and control to continuous integration, packaging, and deployment.

You will examine these properties and behaviors; you will also look at both the benefits and the challenges of this microservice approach. Along with this examination, you will learn how to identify microservices and how to determine where the seams and boundaries are within the domains you are working in.

Autonomous and Isolated

- **Autonomous**: Existing or capable of existing independently; responding, reacting, or developing independently of the whole.

- **Isolated**: Separate from others, happening in different places and at different times.

Microservices are autonomous and isolated. That means that microservices are self-contained units of functionally with loosely coupled dependencies on other services and are designed, developed, tested, and released independently.

Implications

For the past several years, we have been developing standards and practices for team development of large, complex systems using a layered, monolithic architecture. This is reflected in how we organize into teams, structure our solutions and source code control systems, and package and release our software.

Monolithic solutions are built, tested, and deployed as one large body of code, typically across set of server or VM instances, in order to provide scale and performance. If a bug is fixed or a feature added or content updated, the entire solution is built, tested, and deployed across the server farm as one large entity. The process of building, deploying, and regression testing the monolith is costly and time-consuming. Over time, these monoliths turn into large, complex, tightly coupled systems that are nearly impossible to maintain and evolve in new directions.

If you want to adopt a microservices architecture, your standards and practices will need to adapt to this new pattern. Teams will need to be organized in such a way as to support the development of microservices as distinct, independent products. The development, test, and production environments will need to be organized to support these teams, developing and deploying their microservice products separate of one another. When changes are made, only the microservice affected needs to go through the deployment pipeline, thus simplifying the process of updating the system and delivering new features and functions.

By dividing the solution up into its microservice component parts and treating them as separate development efforts, the speed of development will increase and the cost of making changes will go down.

Elastic, Resilient, and Responsive

- **Elastic**: Capable of returning to its original length, shape, etc., after being stretched, deformed, compressed, or expanded.

- **Resilient**: Able to become strong, healthy, or successful again after something bad happens.

- **Responsive**: Quick to respond or react.

Microservices are reused across many different solutions and therefore must be able to scale appropriately depending on the usage scenario. They must be fault-tolerant and provide a reasonable timeframe for recovery if something does go awry. Finally, they need to be responsive, providing reasonable performance given the execution scenario.

Implications

The environment in which you deploy your microservices must provide dynamic scale and high availability configurations for both stateful and stateless services. This is achieved by leveraging a modern cloud platform such as Microsoft Azure.

Azure provides all the necessary capabilities to support elastic scale, fault tolerance, and high availability as well as configuration options that allow you the right size for performance. You will delve into how Azure is a microservices platform in greater detail in Chapter 4.

Message-Oriented and Programmable

Message-Oriented: Software that connects separate systems in a network by carrying and distributing messages between them.

Programmable: A plan of tasks that are done in order to achieve a specific result.

Microservices rely on APIs and data contracts to define how interaction with the service is achieved. The API defines a set of network-visible endpoints, and the data contract defines the structure of the message that is either sent or returned.

Implications

Defining service end points and data contracts is not new. Microservice architecture builds on the evolution of industry standards to define the interaction semantics. If these standards evolve or new ones are introduced, a microservice architecture will evolve to adopt these new standards.

At the time of this writing, the industry has generally settled on Representational State Transfer (ReST) over HTTP for defining API endpoints and JavaScript Object Notation (JSON) for the definition of data contracts. In addition, service bus capabilities such as store and forward message queues are used to provide loose coupling between components and an asynchronous programming model.

APIs and data contracts are the outermost edge of a microservice and define how a client of the service can invoke a function. Behind this API may be a very sophisticated set of software components, storage mediums, and multiple VM instances that provide the function. To the consumer of the service this is all a black box, meaning they know the published inputs and outputs but nothing else about the inner workings. As a consumer of that service, they have knowledge of the published inputs and outputs, and nothing more. What is expected is that a message is constructed, the API is invoked, and a response is returned. The interaction between the consumer and the service is finite and distinct.

Configurable

> **Configurable**: To design or adapt to form a specific configuration or for some specific purpose.

Microservices must provide more than just an API and a data contract. They must also be configurable. Each microservice will have different levels of configuration, and the act of configuring may take different forms. The key point, in order to be reusable and be able to address the needs of each system that chooses to employ its capabilities, is that a microservice must provide a means by which it can be appropriately molded to the usage scenario.

Implications

As you begin the design process for a microservice, you will soon discover that multiple APIs will emerge. Along with the public-facing API that you want to expose to the world, other endpoints will surface that are more of an administrative function and will be used to define how to bootstrap, monitor, manage, scale, configure, and perform other perfunctory operations on the service.

Like any good software product, a microservice should provide an easy-to-use interface or console for administrative functions to configure and manage running instances. Behind the console is, of course, a set of private to semi-private APIs that provides access to the underlying data and configuration settings driving the service.

A microservice, then, is more than just its public-facing ReST API and consists of multiple APIs with varying levels of access, supporting administrative consoles and a runtime infrastructure to support all of the above. It is a software product with all the trimmings.

Automated

> **Automated**: Having controls that allow something to work or happen without being directly controlled by a person.

The lifecycle of a microservice should be fully automated, from design all the way through deployment.

Implications

As you ponder this new world of software product development made up of microservices, it may occur to you that this whole effort could be quite complex with a proliferation of independent microservice products and all the complexity that entails, and you would not be wrong.

This approach should not be undertaken without first having complete automated control over the software development lifecycle. This is about having the right set of tools to support a fully automated development pipeline, but more importantly it is about evolving to a DevOps culture.

A DevOps culture is one that promotes collaboration and integration of the development and operations teams. When you form a team that is responsible for the design, implementation, and deployment of a microservice, that team should be cross functional, consisting of all the skills necessary to carry the process from design through deployment. That means that traditional development teams consisting of architects, developers, and testers should be expanded to include operations.

While developers are traditionally responsible for the automation from build through test, called continuous integration, the operations group is traditionally responsible for deployment across test, staging, and production. Combining these teams offers the opportunity to make automation of the entire product development pipeline as well as the monitoring, diagnostics, and recovery operations a first class activity of the product team. This process is called automation, and the entire team takes responsibility for smooth operation of product releases.

The Benefits of Microservices

Now that you have a working definition of microservices, let's examine the benefits of this approach to distributed computing.

Evolutionary

The days of big bang software product development are over. It is no longer possible to go on a multi-month or multi-year development cycle before releasing a product because by the time you release, the window of opportunity has passed and your competition has already been there, done that.

You may find yourself responsible for the ongoing maintenance and development of an existing, complex, monolithic system made up of millions of lines of code. There will be no stomach for the complete re-implementation of such a system; the business could not sustain it.

One of the benefits of microservice architecture is that you can evolve towards this approach one service at a time, identifying a business capability, implementing it as a microservice, and integrating using a loose coupling pattern, with the existing monolith providing a bridge to the new architecture.

Over time, more and more capabilities can be migrated, shrinking the scope of the monolith until it is just a husk of its original form. The move to microservices will open the door to new user experiences and new business opportunities.

Open

Microservices are designed to expose their functionality through industry standards for network-addressable APIs and data contracts, and are hosted on highly scalable, elastic, resilient cloud platforms. This allows a microservice team to choose the programming language, operating system, and data store that best fits the needs of their service and their skill set without worrying about interoperability.

It is possible to have some microservice teams developing in Node.JS, others in Java, and still others in C#. All those microservices can be used together in one solution because the composition is happening at the ReST API level.

This can be a tremendous improvement for teams that are distributed around the world and currently trying to work together on a monolithic solution. By creating cross-functional teams in each geography and giving them complete responsibility over specific microservices, the need to coordinate around the clock goes away and is replaced with coordination at the API layer, which is not time-bound.

High Velocity

Individual microservices have a small surface area of functionality. With one team responsible for the development lifecycle and all the various components, technology, and automation that make up its implementation, the velocity at which a microservice can be designed, developed, deployed, and updated is magnitudes faster than trying to perform the same operations across a monolithic solution.

Reusable and Composable

Microservices by their very nature are reusable. They are not beholden to any one solution. They are independent entities providing a business or platform capability and exposing that functionality through open internet standards.

In order to create a useful solution for an end user, multiple microservices can be composed together. These user experiences can be implemented as web and mobile applications or targeting new devices such as wearables that may become popular in the future.

Flexible

The deployment of a microservice is defined through its automation. By defining deployment and scale scenarios through automation tools, the Microservice team can exert a great deal of control. There is a tremendous amount of flexibility in how the service moves through development, test, staging, and production and, when in production, how they can be modified to fit different usage scenarios through configuration.

Automation of deployment and scale configurations will provide the necessary control of defining the runtime environment from the container in which the service runs, the instances onto which those containers are deployed, the geographical regions into which those instances are instantiated, and the elastic configurations that define scale.

Versionable and Replaceable

Since there is complete control over the deployment scenarios for a microservice, it becomes possible to have multiple versions of a service running side by side, providing backward compatibility and easy migration.

Versioning is typically handled at the API level where version numbers are integrated into the URL. A new version of the microservice API can be released without impacting clients that are using previous versions of the API. It is also possible to provide ongoing updates and enhancements to existing services while in production.

Using this approach, services can be fully replaced while maintaining the current API or new implementations can be released under a new version.

Owned by One Team

As mentioned, a microservice architecture approach requires organizing cross-functional teams for the purpose of owning the microservice product lifecycle from design through deployment. If you are down the path of adopting Agile Principles and the Scrum Process, you are well suited to adopt this architecture pattern.

The Challenges of Microservices

Just as in the past when you made changes in the way you designed and developed software, a move to Microservices will not be without its challenges. Go in with both your eyes and your mind wide open.

[re]Organization

Organizing to support a microservice architecture approach is one of the most difficult challenges you will have. If you are part of a command-and-control organization using a waterfall software project management approach, you will struggle because you are not oriented to high-velocity product development. If you lack a DevOps culture and there is no collaboration between development and operations to automate the deployment pipeline, you will struggle.

If you are looking for an opportunity to adopt this approach, it is recommended that you not try to make large, sweeping changes to your organization. Instead, look for an opportunity within the context of a business initiative to test out this new formula and then follow these steps:

- Form a small cross-functional team.

- Provide training and guidance on adopting Agile, Scrum, Azure, and microservice architecture.

- Provide a separate physical location for this team to work so that they are not adversely effected by internal politics and old habits.

- Take a minimal-viable-product approach and begin to deliver small incremental releases of one microservice, taking the process all the way through the lifecycle.

- Integrate this service with the existing systems using a loosely coupled approach.

- Go through the lifecycle on this microservice several times until you feel comfortable with the process.

- Put the core team into leadership positions as you form new cross-functional teams to disseminate the knowledge.

Platform

Creating the runtime environment for microservices requires a significant investment in dynamic infrastructure across regionally disperse data centers. If your current on-premises application platform does not support automation, dynamic infrastructure, elastic scale, and high availability, then it makes sense to consider a cloud platform.

Microsoft Azure is a microservice platform, and it provides a fully automated dynamic infrastructure, SDKs, and runtime containers along with a large portfolio of existing microservices that you can leverage, such as DocumentDb, Redis In-Memory Cache, and Service Bus, to build your own microservices catalog.

Identification

Domain-driven design was introduced by Eric Evans in his book by the same title. Eric outlined an approach to describing domain models made up of entities; their attributes, roles, and relationships; and the bounded contexts, the areas of business capability where these models are applied.

From a well-articulated, domain-driven design, you can formulate a layered architecture that will provide the framework for a monolithic solution (see Figure 2-1).

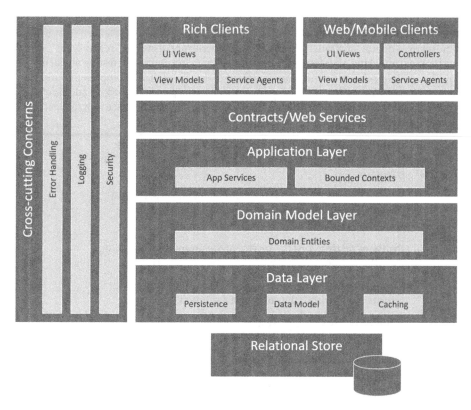

Figure 2-1. *Layered Architecture*

Domain-driven design has served us well and survived the test of time. Domain modeling is still a relevant technique we can use in the age of microservices. Instead of mapping our models and bounded contexts to a layered architecture, we can instead find the seams and separate each bounded context along with its model and use that as the starting point for a microservice architecture.

If you are currently working with a complex layered architecture and have a reasonable domain model defined, the domain model will provide a roadmap to an evolutionary approach to migrating to a microservice architecture.

If a domain model does not exist, you can apply domain-driven design in reverse to identify the bounded contexts, the capabilities within the system. Look for areas of the system where the language changes; this is a design seam. These seams define the boundaries of possible candidates for microservices.

You can also look for areas of the system that are changing rapidly, a lot of refactoring is going on, or the rate of change is very slow and system components are solid. These areas may make a good candidates for microservices.

Finally, those areas of the system that are causing the most pain may be good candidates as well a therapeutic exercise as you cleave off the affected appendage and replace it with a bright, shiny, new microservice.

17

Testing

Microservices do not alter much about the way we write and test code. Test-driven development, mocking, unit testing, functional testing, and regression testing are all in play. We are doing object-oriented development of service-oriented components, and all the best practices, techniques, and tools we used in the past still apply. In addition to these traditional testing mechanisms, we need to test the microservice as it moves through the deployment pipeline.

Internals Testing: Test the internal functions of the service including use of data access, caching, and other cross-cutting concerns.

Service Testing: Test the service implementation of the API. This is a private internal implementation of the API and its associated models.

Protocol Testing: Test the service at the protocol level, calling the API over the specified wire protocol, usually HTTP(s).

Composition Testing: Test the service in collaboration with other services within the context of a solution.

Scalability/Throughput Testing: Test the scalability and elasticity of the deployed microservice.

Failover/Fault Tolerance Testing: Test the ability of the microservice to recover after a failure.

PEN Testing: Work with a third-party software security firm to perform penetration testing. NOTE: This will requires cooperation with Microsoft if you are pen testing microservices deployed to Azure.

Like automation, testing of a microservice through each phase of the deployment pipeline is critical to delivering quality software at velocity. Careful planning, discipline, and a team approach to testing will make this aspect of adopting microservices run smoothly.

Discoverability

Locating services in a distributed environment can be handled in three ways:

- **Hardcode the locations of the microservices and deal with all the issues that will arise when services move or fail with or without notice**: This is akin to hardcoding a database connection string or user id and password. It's not a good idea.

- **Leverage file-based or runtime environment-based configuration mechanisms to store and retrieve the microservice locations**: This is a good choice if combined with an automated process to update when locations change.

- **Provide a dynamic location microservice for microservices so that applications and services can look up the current location at runtime**: This lookup service may also provide health checks and notices if services are failing or performing poorly.

In order to provide discoverability as a service, it may require either acquiring a third-party product, integrating an open source solution, or building it yourself. You will examine a custom discoverability microservice called ConfigM that provides dynamic location and metadata services for microservices running in your deployment environments including test, staging, and production.

Summary

Microservices do one thing and they do it well.

They represent business capabilities defined using domain-driven design, implemented using object-oriented best practices, tested at each step in the deployment pipeline, and deployed through automation as autonomous, isolated, highly scalable, resilient services in a distributed cloud infrastructure. They are owned by a single team that approaches the development of a microservice as a product, delivering high-quality software in an iterative, high-velocity process with customer involvement and satisfaction as the key metrics of success.

In the next chapter, we will compare layered and microservice architectures, and delve into the internal structure of a microservice.

CHAPTER 3

■ ■ ■

Microservice Architecture

Separation of Concerns, even if not perfectly possible, is yet the only available technique for effective ordering of one's thoughts that I know of.

—Edsger W. Dijkstra

Separation of Concerns (SoC) is a design principle for separating implementation into distinct layers such that each layer addresses a separate concern. Separation of Concerns is achieved through the combination of information encapsulation and well-defined interfaces for accessing that information. We have been applying separation of concerns since the earliest days of programming. Functional programming was born out of this approach and we have been reapplying this principle as we have evolved the tools, languages, and architectures ever since.

Layered architecture applies SoC to identify the horizontal seams between presentation, application, and data tiers. This process is then continued within each tier of the architecture. The presentation tier can use the Model-View-Controller (MVC) pattern to define a separation of concerns for the user interface implementation. MVC defines three cooperating components: the model, the view, and the controller. The model defines the behavior, rules, and business logic, and manages the data of an application. A view is the component that is responsible for displaying the model. There can be multiple views in an application because the data can be displayed in various forms such as tables, charts, lists, etc. The controller accepts user input and converts it to commands for the model or view. This is a great example of Separation of Concerns.

Microservices architecture uses SoC to find the seams in a domain-driven design, identifying business capabilities and cross-cutting concerns, each designed implemented, tested, and deployed as autonomous, isolated services. This chapter compares layered and microservices architecture, and looks at how the Separation of Concerns principle is used to create a logical architecture for a microservices solution as well as the internal architecture of an individual microservice.

Layered Architecture

A layered architecture uses a separation of concerns to provide a roadmap for the implementation of both simple and complex applications. Consider the 3-tier architecture, a logical separation between user experience (presentation layer), business capabilities (application layer), and persistence (data layer), as shown in Figure 3-1.

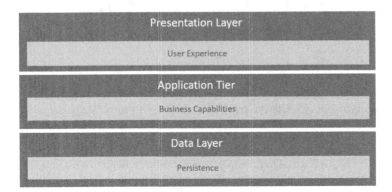

Figure 3-1. *3-Tier Architecture*

When you apply this simple model to real world scenarios, the layers increase in complexity and responsibility. Domain-driven design was introduced, presenting an extensive set of best practices, techniques, and core principles that facilitate system design.

The solutions need to support an evolving client landscape of desktops, browsers, mobile phones, and tablets. Service-oriented architecture was introduced to provide discipline and governance as web services and open standards were adopted to connect these various user experiences to the application layer (see Figure 3-2).

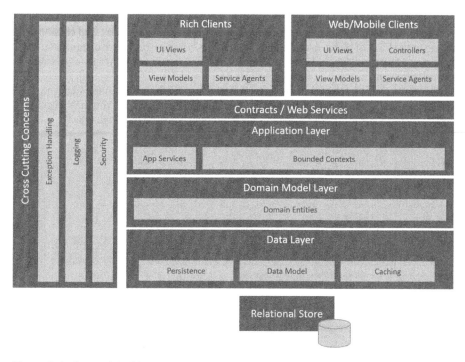

Figure 3-2. *Layered Architecture*

The application layer, accessed using SOAP or ReST, exposed the services and contracts that defined the business capabilities. The domain model layer was added to capture the business rules and the data models, and to encapsulate the in-memory caching, persistence, and transactional nature of the operations provided by the data layer.

When implemented and deployed, all of the server-side functionality was built over one large relational store, and was typically replicated across a farm of load-balanced servers to provide scale and throughput.

As discussed, this approach has some difficulty translating to cloud platforms such as Azure. While it is possible to perform a "lift and shift" of the on-premises workloads to Azure's Infrastructure as a Service environment, we are not able to take full advantage of what the platform has to offer with respect to ease of deployment, elastic scale, and adoption of other platform services. In order to take full advantage of the cloud, we need to take what we have learned and evolve to a new model.

A Microservice Approach

A microservices architecture maintains the logical separation of presentation, business, and data layers. Where microservices architecture departs is from a monolithic application and data layer to a collection of distinct, isolated services. The business and data layers are vertically sliced along functional seams, each with its own domain model and API.

The data services layer is a collection of microservices providing various types of persistence services from caching, document stores, relational databases, and cloud storage in the form of blobs, tables, queues, and disks. These services are instantiated on-demand and provide secure end points that are accessed using an API invoked over a network protocol.

Traditional cross-cutting concerns such as logging, configuration, reference data, and discoverability also exist within this architecture as microservices. You may leverage third-party products for these capabilities or build them yourself (see Figure 3-3).

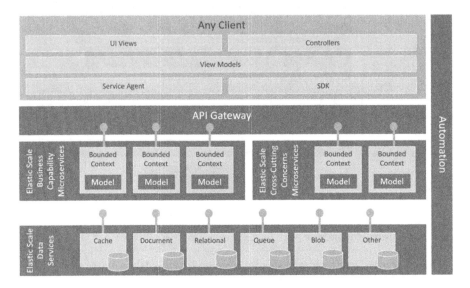

Figure 3-3. *Microservices Architecture*

The business capabilities of the solution are each implemented and deployed as isolated microservices that, in turn, leverage the cross-cutting and data layer microservices.

Desktops, browsers, mobile phones, tablets, wrist watches, and any device we connect to the cloud, such as vending machines, robots, street lamps, industrial machinery, etc. (what we call the Internet of Things), can create user experiences from the provided APIs.

To create a consistent and secure view of the APIs, an API gateway microservice can be employed. Gateways provides registration, subscription, policy injection, documentation, and analytics for your microservice APIs.

Finally, all the microservices that are required for a solution are instantiated, configured, and managed using automation tools and languages. For example, a microservice implemented using Azure may instantiate SQL Database for relational database capabilities, a Service Bus Queue for store and forward capabilities, and an Azure Web site container to host the ReST API. The promise of Continuous Delivery is now possible: the ability to provide ongoing updates and new feature releases at a rapid pace without affecting the entire deployed application.

Microservice Logical Architecture

Fractals are a curved or geometric figure where each part has many characteristics as the whole object. Not unlike fractals, if we peer inside a microservice we will see something that looks very familiar: a layered architecture that is providing a separation of concerns from the client to the data store. Microservices follow the same best practices and approaches to their design as we have applied to large scale monolithic applications, but at a much smaller scale. The difference is that the scope of this architecture is focused on doing one thing and doing that one thing well (see Figure 3-4).

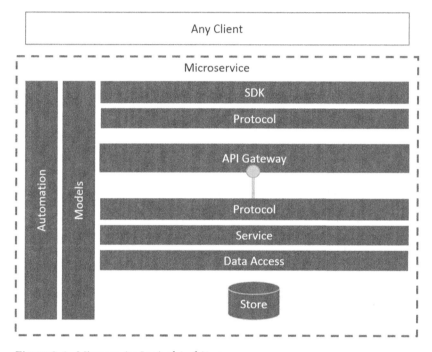

Figure 3-4. *Microservice Logical Architecture*

Models

Models define the structure of data as it moves in and out of a microservice. Data moves in and out of a microservice through the data access and the protocol layers. In both cases, serialization and deserialization is performed. Within the service layer of the microservice, the model takes an in-memory form such as an object model.

For example,

```
class UserProfile
{
        string id { get; set; }
        string first { get; set; }
        string last { get; set; }
}
...
UserProfile user = new UserProfile();

user.id = "99999";
user.first = "Bob";
user.last = "Familiar";
```

defines a simple model for a user profile and instantiates an in-memory instance. An example of this model de-serialized to JSON would look like this:

```
{ "id" : "99999", "first" : "Bob", "last" : "Familiar" }
```

SDK Layer

In order to facilitate easy adoption of an API, it may be desirable to create language-specific SDKs. The SDKs can be made available through package managers such as NuGet to make discoverability and installation relatively painless. NuGet is the package manager for the Microsoft development platform. The NuGet client tools allow you to create and use NuGet packages created from class library solutions. Chapter 5 will cover how to use NuGet to create reusable packages for your class libraries and host them locally in your own build environment.

Note that there is the added overhead of maintaining the SDKs for each supported language. Also with the advancements in API gateway technology, auto-generated sample code and IntelliSense can easily fill the gap of providing documentation and instruction if you opt not to provide SDKs.

API Gateway Layer

API gateways provide a proxy for your API. You register your API with the gateway service and turn features of the gateway on and off through configuration. These features include additional layers of security, subscription services for developers to provide unique keys required on each API invocation, performance metrics and analytics, throttling, policy injection such as XML to JSON or JSON to XML transformations, redirection, and other filtering operations. The API Management Service provides these services in Azure.

Protocol Layer

The protocol layer defines the network protocol and communication mechanism that will be used by the microservice, such as HTTP or TCP for the network protocol and SOAP/WSDL or ReST for the communication mechanism.

As discussed, the predominant protocol and communication style today is ReST over HTTP with JSON as the preferred message format. JSON has replaced XML due to its more compact format and object-oriented notation.

ReST APIs are defined as a collection of URLs and corresponding HTTP VERBS along with input and output parameters and messages. Each URL consists of the network protocol (HTTP), a base URL (myapi.looksfamilar.com), and the route to the resource along with any parameters.

There are two ways to specify parameters on a URL. The first way uses the resource path format to return the user profile with the user id 99999 in JSON format.

GetProfilesById

```
GET http://myapi.looksfamiliar.com/profiles/user/id/99999
```

The second technique uses the query parameters URL format to return all user profiles whose location is set to Massachusetts as a list formatted as a JSON array.

GetProfilesByLocation

```
GET http://myapi.looksfamiliar.com/profiles?location=Massachusetts
```

POST and PUT operations will typically require a JSON message as input. The format of the JSON is based on the model for that microservice. For example, if you defined an API for the creation of a user profile, the URL would be defined as

```
POST http://myapi.looksfamiliar.com/profiles/user
```

and the message would be passed as content with the format of

```
{ "id" : "99999", "first" : "Bob", "last" : "Familiar" }
```

The protocol layer performs the routing of these incoming HTTP requests to the appropriate function provided by the service layer.

Service Layer

The service layer is where the actual work happens. This part of the architecture defines the business rules, workflows, calculations, and any other operation required to provide the implementation of the microservice. This layer leverages the data access layer for persistence, caching, and other data-oriented operations.

Taking the simple example introduced above, an implementation of the protocol layer for GetProfileById using ASP.NET Web API would look like this:

```
[Route("profile/users/id/{id}")]
[HttpGet]
public UserProfile GetById(string id)
{
  UserProfileService profileService = new UserProfileService();
  return profileService.GetById(id);
}
```

The Route attribute defines the expected resource path and parameters and the HttpGet attribute defines the supported HTTP Verb. The method defined at the protocol layer uses a class that implements the service called UserProfileService. The protocol layer in this example is very thin so as to offer an easy path to adopting new protocols in the future.

The service implementation sans error handling would look like this:

```
public UserProfile GetById(string id)
{
    UserProfile user = null;
    DataAccess dac = new DataAccess();
    dac.Connect(_connectionString);
    return dac.SelectById<UserProfile>(id);
}
```

An instance of the DataAccess class is instantiated and initialized with a connection string. This class contains a SelectById() method that takes the user Id and returns the UserProfile model for that user.

Data Access Layer

The data access layer encapsulates the use of data layer microservices such as caching, relational, document, and blob stores as well as message queues and other store and forward services.

A common pattern provided by a data access layer is to hide the details of the relationship between the caching services and the persistence store (see Figure 3-5).

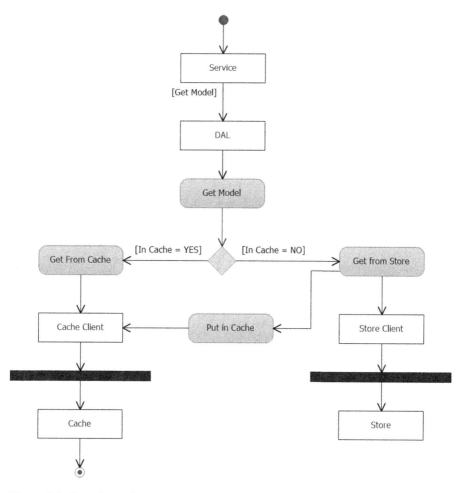

Figure 3-5. *Data Access Layer Get Activity Diagram*

The service requests a model from the data access layer (DAL). The DAL first checks the cache and, if found, returns the model. The call to the cache is done through a cache client that manages the protocol invocation of the cache API. If the model is not found in the cache, the model is retrieved from the store. The call to the store is also done through a store client that manages the protocol invocation of the store API. The model is placed into the cache and returned to the service.

Similarly, when the service wants to save a model, it passes the model to the DAL, which saves to the store using the store client, and then either puts or updates the model in the cache using the cache client (see Figure 3-6).

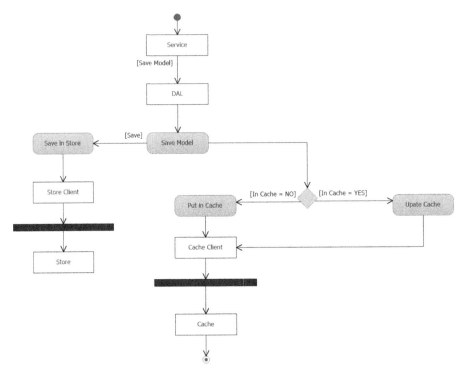

Figure 3-6. *Data Access Layer Save Activity Diagram*

Store

There are many storage options when leveraging a cloud platform such as Microsoft Azure. Each one is offered as a microservice that can be instantiated, configured, scaled, secured, and automated to meet your needs. Later in this book, you will take a close look at SQL Database, DocumentDb, Redis Cache, Service Bus Queues and Event Hubs, Stream Analytics, and Azure Blobs and Tables.

Automation

The automation component of the microservice architecture is the recognition that the approach outlined in this book is not possible without the ability to automate the development lifecycle of a microservices-based solution. There is a level of complexity that is introduced with this approach because the entire solution involves many moving parts and components. Trying to manually manage change in this world is impossible. Tools such as PowerShell, Chef, and Puppet need to be considered along with the addition of operations expertise to the team.

A DevOps culture is one where teams are made up of cross-functional skillsets; they contain all the skills necessary to design, implement, test, deploy, and maintain software. This means that developers and operations engineers work together, side by side, throughout the entire product lifecycle. The smooth operation of the practice of software development becomes everyone's responsibility. Like the workers on an assembly line in a lean manufacturing shop, a breakdown in the flow from one station to another stops the entire line. It is everyone's job to determine what the problem is and how to fix it before the line starts up again.

The roles, responsibilities, tools, and languages used to implement automation are choices left up to the team. No single tool or language can solve this issue. Each step in the process may be implemented using a different tool or scripting language, selected and maintained by the team as a whole. Automation is never 100%. The goal should be to automate the process as much as possible to guarantee consistency, quality, stability, and data collection for measuring progress and success.

Summary

The progression from layered monolithic to microservices is not such a leap. It is simply the evolution of the concept of Separation of Concerns, a design principle for separating implementation into distinct layers, such that each layer addresses a separate concern. SoC is achieved through the combination of encapsulation and well-defined interfaces.

Microservices architecture uses SoC to find the seams in a domain-driven design in order to identify business capabilities and cross-cutting concerns. Each capability and concern is then designed, implemented, tested, and deployed as an autonomous, isolated service.

Now that you have the definition of what you want to build, the next chapter will take a deeper look at the platform, Microsoft Azure, and its capabilities, providing the foundation for your own microservices.

CHAPTER 4

▓ ▓ ▓

Azure, A Microservice Platform

Let's examine Azure with respect to our definition of microservices:

- Azure Services are isolated and autonomous: Yes

- Azure Services are configurable: Yes

- Azure Services provide elastic scale: Yes

- Azure Services are programmable through secure endpoints: Yes

- Azure Services are automatable through a ReST API such that the creation, management, monitoring, and teardown is controlled completely through software: Yes

- Azure Services are composable in that they can be combined in uncountable ways to formulate solutions that address business and technical goals: Yes

Azure's finished services such as SQL Database, Service Bus, or DocumentDB, exhibit characteristics of microservices because they themselves are designed and implemented using a Microservice Architecture. Each finished service consists of several microservices each providing a distinct capability. If you approach Azure as a platform optimized for microservices, you will be able to extract the most value from the platform for your solutions.

At the time of this writing, Azure has 11 service categories, each with multiple finished services providing a plethora of capability:

- **Compute**: Virtual Machines, Cloud Services, Remote App, and Batch

- **Web and Mobile**: Web, Mobile, API and Logic Apps, API Management, Notification Hubs, Mobile Services

- **Data and Storage**: SQL Database, DocumentDb, Redis Cache, Storage, StorSimple, Search

- **Analytics and IoT**: HDInsight, Machine Learning, Stream Analytics, Data Factory, Event Hubs, SQL Data Warehouse

- **Networking**: Virtual Network, Express Route, Traffic Manager, Load Balancer, DNS, VPN Gateway

- **Media and CDN**: Media Services, Encoding, Media Player, Media Intelligence, Content Protection, Live and On-Demand Streaming, Content Delivery Network (CDN)

- **Hybrid Integration**: Service Bus, BizTalk Services, Backup, Site Recovery

- **Identify and Access Management**: Active Directory, Multi-Factor Authentication

- **Developer Services and Management**: Visual Studio Online (VSO), Application Insights

- **Management**: Key Vault, Scheduler, Automation, Operational Insights

The Microsoft Azure team has adopted a lean engineering, Agile approach to how they develop their microservices and they use a Continuous Delivery deployment process to provide early access to new services (Preview) and updates to existing services at a rapid pace. If you think Azure is missing some capability, like the weather in New England, just wait 15 minutes.

In this chapter, you will look at several Azure finished services, and learn how to instantiate, configure, and develop code to use these services. You will look at storage services such as Azure Storage, SQL Database, DocumentDb, and Redis Cache; messaging services provided by Service Bus; the API gateway service API Management; and deployment containers Cloud Services and App Services.

What will emerge is a pattern that you will want to carry forward in the development of your own microservices; the ability to automate the creation of your services, the ability to expose both a programmable API as well as a management API using ReST, and architecting your services so that they can scale elastically. By examining these Azure services, you will be able to leverage this approach for your own microservices and take full advantage of Azure for your Software as a Service solutions.

Data and Storage

Data and storage services give you options on how you persist, transact, and cache your data. Each service has its own characteristics and use cases.

Azure Storage

Azure Storage is a service that provides storage and retrieval of petabytes of highly available unstructured data. There are four types of Azure Storage:

- **Blobs**: Binary Large Objects, such as documents and media, useful for storage of any kind of file.

- **Tables**: NoSQL-like data, useful for scaling up without having to shard (creating horizontal partitions in the data store).

- **Queues**: Reliable messaging, useful for loose coupling of applications.

- **Files**: Managed file share, useful for simulating a disk drive.

You can program these storage services using ReST or leverage a client SDK. The architecture of Azure storage, depicted in Figure 4-1, provides a common scale out, load balancing, and indexing capability which manages partitioning. That layer is in turn built on a distributed replication layer which provides both Locally Redundant Storage (LRS), which creates three copies of the data, and Geographically Redundant Storage (GRS), which creates six copies of the data.

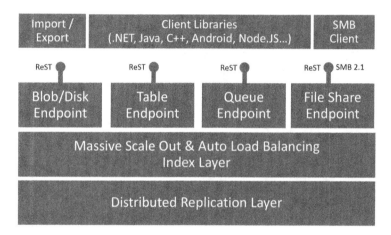

Figure 4-1. *Azure Storage Architecture*

To get started, first you create a storage account in Azure.

1. In the preview portal, click the New button in the upper left corner (see Figure 4-2).

2. Select Data + Storage from the menu.

3. Select Storage.

4. Fill out the form supplying a unique name, pricing tier, resource group, subscription, and location, and then click Create.

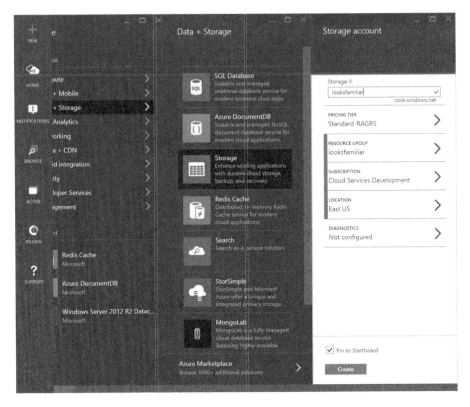

Figure 4-2. *Creating an Azure storage account*

Once the storage account is created, navigate to the storage account screen and click the key icon to access the connection string (see Figure 4-3).

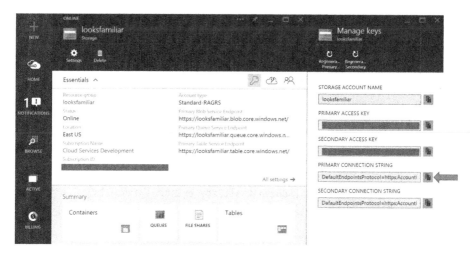

Figure 4-3. *Managing keys for an Azure storage account*

Now you are ready to programmatically access the new storage account. Place the connection string in the `app.config` or `web.config` of your solution and install the Azure Storage Client SDK using the NuGet Package Manager (see Figure 4-4).

Figure 4-4. *Installing Azure Storage NuGet package*

Add references to the Azure Storage namespaces as appropriate to be able to use the Blob, Table, Queue, or File clients.

```
using Microsoft.WindowsAzure.Storage;
using Microsoft.WindowsAzure.Storage.Auth;
using Microsoft.WindowsAzure.Storage.Blob;
using Microsoft.WindowsAzure.Storage.Table;
using Microsoft.WindowsAzure.Storage.Queue;
using Microsoft.WindowsAzure.Storage.File;
```

Here is an example of how to use the Blob Client to upload a file to storage:

```
// connect to the storage account
CloudStorageAccount storageAccount = CloudStorageAccount.Parse(
    ConfigurationManager.ConnectionStrings["StorageConnStr"]);

// create the blob client.
CloudBlobClient blobClient =  storageAccount.CreateCloudBlobClient();

// retrieve a reference to a container.
CloudBlobContainer container = blobClient.GetContainerReference("mynewcontainer");

// create the container if it doesn't already exist.
container.CreateIfNotExists();

// Create a blob "mynewblob" with contents from a local file.
using (var fileStream = System.IO.File.OpenRead(@"path\myfile"))
{
    blockBlob.UploadFromStream(fileStream);
}
```

As you incorporate storage into your solutions, you will want an easy way to navigate, check status, and add and remove content. There are many tools available, some of which are free of charge, and others cost a nominal fee. Visual Studio provides Azure Storage Explorer as part of the Server Explorer. Azure Storage Explorer is a standalone app and is offered as a free download from CodePlex at http://azurestorageexplorer.codeplex.com/.

Azure Explorer is from Cerebrata and is also standalone and free. Go to www.cerebrata.com/.

Azure Management Studio is a feature-rich tool from Cerebrata (see Figure 4-5). It includes a 30-day trial for you to check out its advanced capabilities.

Figure 4-5. *Azure Management Studio from Cerebrata*

SQL Database

SQL Database provides a relational database as a managed service. It is based on the Microsoft SQL Server engine and supports existing tools, libraries, and APIs, which is great if you are looking to leverage existing data access code.

SQL Database is configurable to provide both scale up as well as scale out configurations. It also provides auditing, restore, geo-replication, and point-in-time restore from any transaction up to 35 days.

To provision an instance of SQL Database, go to the Azure Portal (`https://portal.azure.com`), log in, and click New ➤ Data + Storage ➤ SQL Database (see Figure 4-6). Fill out the form, providing a name for the server, login credentials, and optionally the name of a default database.

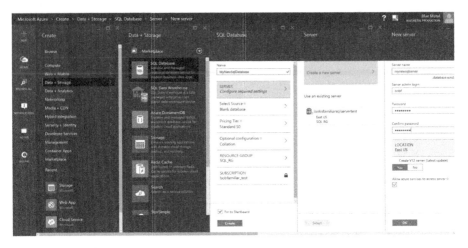

Figure 4-6. *Provisioning SQL Database*

Once the SQL Database is instantiated, visit the "classic" portal at `http://manage.azure.com`, configure the firewall rules and your IP address, and retrieve the database connection strings (see Figure 4-7).

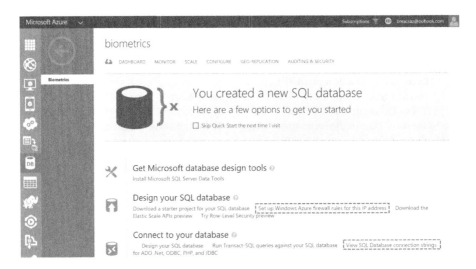

Figure 4-7. *SQL Database Firewall and Connection Settings*

You can use the same tools you use today for on-premises SQL Server instances to access, manage, and develop, including SQL Server Management Studio and Visual Studio.

DocumentDb

NoSQL has emerged as an alternative to relational databases to provide a more agile data store that maps nicely to the high-velocity development processes in use today. It eliminates the impedance mismatch between application object models and the database because JSON serialization is used to produce both the on-the-wire communication and the storage format.

DocumentDb provides tunable consistency with the ability to choose from four levels:

- **Strong**: Guarantees that a write is only visible after the group of replica DocumentDb services all agree that the write has been committed; this provides the best guarantee on data consistency, but offers the lowest level of performance.

- **Bounded-staleness**: Guarantees success of all writes but does not guarantee that reads will keep pace with these updates; provides predictable behavior for read operations while offering lowest latency writes.

- **Session**: Guarantees individual reads and writes, and the ability to read your own writes; provides predictable read operations while offering low latency writes.

- **Eventual**: The weakest form of consistency wherein a client may get values that are older than the ones it had seen before; provides the weakest read consistency but offers the lowest latency for both reads and writes.

These well-defined, granular consistency levels allow you to make sound trade-offs between consistency, availability, and latency. You instantiate an instance of the DocumentDb by visiting the portal and clicking New ➤ Data + Storage ➤ Azure DocumentDb (see Figure 4-8).

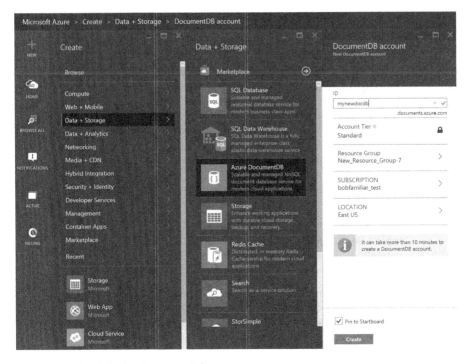

Figure 4-8. *Provisioning DocumentDb*

You can define one or more databases within the context of the DocumentDb instance. Each database can have one or more collections. Collections can contain documents in JSON format, and stored procedures, triggers, and user-defined functions (UDF) written in JavaScript (see Figure 4-9).

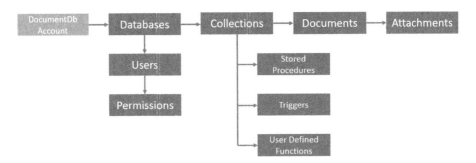

Figure 4-9. *DocumentDb Internal Structure*

42

DocumentDb is a schema-free database system. It does not require any schema for the JSON documents. As you add documents to a collection, DocumentDb automatically indexes them and they are available to query. As with all Azure Services, you can program DocumentDb using its ReST API or leverage one of the many language SDKs.

Once DocumentDb is instantiated, you can retrieve the URI and security key values from the Key blade on the Azure Preview Portal. These values are used to connect to DocumentDb (see Figure 4-10).

Figure 4-10. *DocumentDb Keys*

Querying DocumentDb is done using Structured Query Language (SQL) over the hierarchical JSON documents. Say you have a reference data collection in DocumentDb with JSON documents that are formatted like this:

```
{
  "id": "dfe49be8-5bd2-4eb0-8bb7-ef1c4b361936",
  "cachettl": 1,
  "domain": "States",
  "code": "AL",
  "codevalue": "Alabama",
  "link": "US",
  "sequence": 0,
  "attributes": [
    {
      "key": "Capitol",
      "val": "Montgomery"
    },
```

```
  {
    "key": "Population",
    "val": "4779736"
  },
  {
    "key": "Square Miles",
    "val": "52419"
  }
  ],
}
```

Creating a query that retrieves all states in a reference data collection would look like this:

```
SELECT * FROM Entity e where e.domain='States'
```

You could also get the same result knowing that the first element in the attributes array has a key value of 'Capitol':

```
SELECT * FROM Entity e where e.attributes[0].key='Capitol'
```

If you want to look up the reference entity for the United States, the query would look like this:

```
SELECT * FROM Entity e where e.code='US'
```

And the JSON returned would be as follows:

```
{
    "id": "6fa6150d-5a83-44e6-95eb-5e299b29e89a",
    "cachettl": 1,
    "domain": "CountryCodes",
    "code": "US",
    "codevalue": "UNITED STATES",
    "link": "",
    "sequence": 0,
    "attributes": [
      {
        "key": "ICO",
        "val": "USA"
      }
    ],
  }
```

To leverage DocumentDb from .NET, you need to reference the Azure DocumentDb Client using NuGet in Visual Studio (see Figure 4-11).

Figure 4-11. *Installing the DocumentDb NuGet package*

Here is an example of how to connect and query DocumentDb using the client SDK. First, you create a class that encapsulates connecting to DocumentDb and provides a generic select by id method. You will call this class DocDb.

```
using Microsoft.Azure.Documents;
using Microsoft.Azure.Documents.Client;
using Microsoft.Azure.Documents.Linq;

namespace LooksFamiliar.Microservice.Store
{
    public class Dbase : IDbase
    {
        private string _docdburi;
        private string _docdbkey;
        private DocumentClient _client;
        private Database _database;
        private DocumentCollection _collection;

        public Dbase(string docdburi, string docdbkey)
        {
            _docdburi = docdburi;
            _docdbkey = docdbkey;
        }

        public void Connect(string databaseId, string collectionId)
        {
            try
            {
                _client = new DocumentClient(new Uri(_docdburi), _docdbkey);
                GetOrCreateDatabaseAsync(databaseId).Wait();
                GetOrCreateCollectionAsync(_database.SelfLink,
                                           collectionId).Wait();
            }
```

```
                catch (Exception err)
                {
                    throw new Exception(Errors.ERR_DBASE_DOCUMENTDB_CONN, err);
                    ;
                }
            }

        private async Task<Database> GetOrCreateDatabaseAsync(string id)
        {
            _database = _client.CreateDatabaseQuery()
                    .Where(db => db.Id == id).ToArray().FirstOrDefault();
            if (_database != null) return _database;
            _database = await _client.CreateDatabaseAsync(new Database {Id = id});
            return _database;
        }

        private async Task<DocumentCollection> GetOrCreateCollectionAsync
        (string dbLink, string id)
        {
            _collection = _client.CreateDocumentCollectionQuery(dbLink)
                    .Where(c => c.Id == id).ToArray().FirstOrDefault();
            if (_collection != null) return _collection;
            _collection = await _client.CreateDocumentCollectionAsync(
                    dbLink, new DocumentCollection {Id = id});
            return _collection;
        }

        public List<T> SelectByQuery<T>(string query)
        {
            var modelList = _client.CreateDocumentQuery<T>(_collection.
            SelfLink, query);
            return modelList.ToList().Select(item => (T) item).ToList();
        }
    }
}
```

Now that you have a class that will handle data access to DocumentDb, you just need to define a class that you want to save and restore as a JSON document. For your reference data, you will define a class called Entity.

■ **Note**   The Entity class defines an id property that is initialized with a GUID formatted as a string. The id field gives you the ability to query specific instances of objects from DocumentDb. In addition, the class defines a cachettl (cache time-to-live) field that is used in conjunction with Redis Cache to define how long the object lives in cache before being automatically removed.

```
    public class Entity
    {
        public Entity()
        {
            id = Guid.NewGuid().ToString();
            cachettl = 1;
        }
        [JsonProperty(PropertyName = "id")]
        public string id { get; set; }
        public int cachettl { get; set; }
        public string domain { get; set; }
        public string code { get; set; }
        public string codevalue { get; set; }
        public string link { get; set; }
        public SEQUENCETYPE sequence { get; set; }
        public List<Attribute> attributes { get; set; }
    }

    public class Attribute
    {
        public Attribute()
        {
            key = string.Empty;
            val = string.Empty;
        }

        public Attribute(string _key, string _val)
        {
            key = _key;
            val = _val;
        }

        public string key { get; set; }
        public string val { get; set; }
    }
}
```

Now that you have your data access class, DocDb, and your model, Entity, assuming you have a DocumentDb collection of reference data, you can query a list of State entities from the reference collection database:

```
// connect to documentdb
var dac = new DocDb();
dac.Connect("MyDocumentDb", "RefCollection");

// initialize the query to select the
// 50 reference entities for the US states
var query = "SELECT * FROM Entity e where e.domain='States'";
```

```
// retrieve a list of states from the reference store
var states = dac.SelectByQuery<Entity>(query);
foreach (Entity state in states)
{
    // do amazing stuff here
}
```

Redis Cache

Microsoft Azure Redis Cache is based on the popular open source Redis Cache. Microsoft Azure Redis Cache provides an in-memory cache service that is accessible using its ReST API or a client SDK (see Figure 4-12).

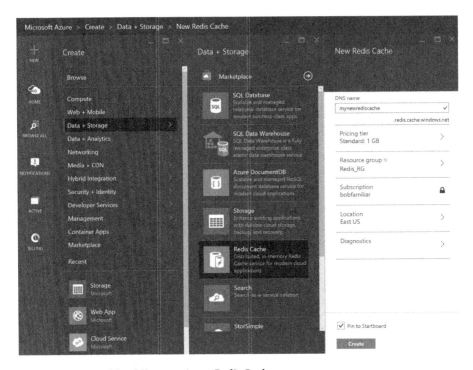

Figure 4-12. *Provision Microsost Azure Redis Cache*

To use Azure Redis Cache from .NET, you reference the StackExchange.Redis client library using NuGet within Visual Studio (see Figure 4-13).

Figure 4-13. *Install StackExchange.Redis NuGet Package*

Once you have created your Redis Cache instance in Azure, you can retrieve the connection information, which is a combination of the URI and the security key. These values together form the connection string:

```
string redisConn =  "[your-account].redis.cache.windows.net,
ssl=true,password=[your-key]";
```

Redis is used by applications to store serialized instances of object models in memory in order to improve access and avoid disk I/O. Since you are standardizing on JSON, the objects you place in cache are first serialized to JSON format and then stored. When they are retrieved, they are de-serialized from JSON to an in-memory object. Each object is referenced in cache using a unique id. It is recommended that you incorporate a unique id in your object models.

▪ **Note**   Examples in this book reference the Newtonsoft JSON.NET NuGet package for serialization and deserialization of JSON.

Here is an example of looking up an entity from a reference data store and caching the result using the Redis client SDK:

```
using StackExchange.Redis;
using Newtonsoft.Json;

// connect to documentdb
var dac = new DocDb();
dac.Connect("MyDocumentDb", "RefCollection");

// initialize the query to get the
// reference entity for the United States
var query = "SELECT * FROM Entity e where e.code='US'";

// retrieve the US country entity from the reference store
var countries = dac.SelectByQuery<Entity>(query);
```

49

```
// connect to redis cache
ConnectionMultiplexer redisConnection = ConnectionMultiplexer.
Connect(redisConn);
IDatabase redisCache = redisConnection.GetDatabase();

// serialize the object to JSON
var json = JsonConvert.SerializeObject(countries[0]);

// cache the object passing in unique id, json string and time to live
redisCache.StringSet( countries[0].id,  json, TimeSpan.
FromMinutes(countries[0].cachettl));
```

Within the cache time-to-live period, if another operation wants to check the cache for a particular entity, the application can perform that operation using the Redis Cache StringGet() method. The method will return null if the object is not found.

```
// look up a reference entity in the cache by id
Entity getFromCache(string id)
{
    var json = cache.StringGet(id);
    var entity = JsonConvert.Deserialize<Entity>(json);
    return entity;
}
```

Service Bus

Service Bus provides several technologies for implementing message-oriented patterns and application integration. The first step in using Service Bus is to define a *namespace*. Within a namespace you can create one or more instances of four types of communication mechanisms:

- **Queues**: Provide one-directional communication, acting as a message broker between a sender and a receiver.

- **Topics**: Provide one-directional communication with multiple subscribers; subscribers can use filters to limit the topics.

- **Relays**: Provide bi-directional communication in a pass-through mode; there is no storage of the message.

- **Event Hubs**: Provide high volume telemetry ingress at massive scale, with low latency and high reliability.

Each queue, topic, relay, and event hub is given a name, and that name combined with the namespace creates a unique end point identifier. You can program queues, topics, relays, and event hubs using ReST APIs or client SDKs. Applications that use these Service Bus communication mechanisms do not need to be hosted in Azure; they can run anywhere.

Each Service Bus endpoint is secured using shared access policies. A Shared Access Policy key is sent as part of a ReST invocation for a Service Bus endpoint. The Share Access Policy key specifies a permission level for that endpoint. There are three permissions that you can specify for a key:

- **Send**: The application can send messages to the endpoint.

- **Listen**: The application can listen to the endpoint (i.e. receive messages).

- **Manage**: The application can send, listen, and manage the endpoint.

You can access the Shared Access Policy configuration settings on the Azure Portal by selecting the Configuration tab for a namespace (see Figure 4-14).

sblooksfamiliar

ALL   QUEUES   TOPICS   RELAYS   EVENT HUBS   SCALE   **CONFIGURE**

shared access policies

NAME	PERMISSIONS
RootManageSharedAccessKey	Manage, Send, Listen
NEW POLICY NAME	

shared access key generator

POLICY NAME	RootManageSharedAccessKey
PRIMARY KEY	Regenerate
SECONDARY KEY	Regenerate

Figure 4-14. *Shared Access Policy Definitions*

Using the Shared Access Policy configuration screen, you can created named policies with permissions that allow Send, Listen, or Manage capabilities. Once you configure the shared access policies, you can get the full Service Bus connection string information from the Azure Portal. To view the connection information for Service Bus, click the Connection Information button on the command bar at the bottom of the Azure Portal (see Figure 4-15).

Figure 4-15. *Connection Information*

The Access Connection Information screen will be displayed (see Figure 4-16). You can copy the connection strings from this dialog and use them in your applications and services.

Access connection information

Use this connection information to manage namespace 'mvasbus'. You can also use authorization policies configured here to connect to all entities in this namespace.

SAS ⓘ

NAME	CONNECTION STRING	🔍
RootManageSharedAccessKey	Endpoint=sb://▓▓▓.servicebus.windows.net/;SharedAccessKeyName=RootMana…	
Send	Endpoint=sb://▓▓▓.servicebus.windows.net/;SharedAccessKeyName=Send;Shar…	
Listen	Endpoint=sb://▓▓▓.servicebus.windows.net/;SharedAccessKeyName=Listen;Shar…	
Manage	Endpoint=sb://▓▓▓.servicebus.windows.net/;SharedAccessKeyName=Manage;Sh…	

Figure 4-16. *Service Bus Connection Information*

Queue

Using Service Bus from .NET requires that the endpoint connection string be present in the configuration section of the settings file of the solution. When using Azure Cloud Services, you can store the connection string in the Azure service configuration files (.CSCFG files). For websites or virtual machines, you store your connection string using the app.config or web.config file.

```
<appSettings>
<add key="Microsoft.ServiceBus.ConnectionString"
value="Endpoint=sb://[your-namespace].servicebus.windows.net;
SharedAccessKeyName=Send;SharedAccessKey=[your secret]" />
</appSettings>
```

In order to write code that uses Service Bus, you add a reference to the Service Bus Client SDK (see Figure 4-17).

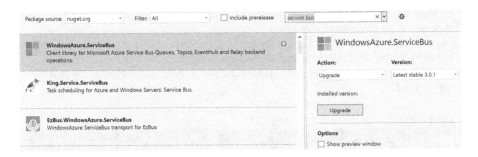

Figure 4-17. *Installing the Service Bus NuGet package*

To send a message to a queue, follow these steps.

1. Define the message you want to send as a class.

2. Create a class that encapsulates connecting, reading, and writing messages.

3. Write the code that uses these classes to send a message to a queue.

This example demonstrates the process outlined above:

```csharp
using Microsoft.ServiceBus;
using Microsoft.ServiceBus.Messaging;
using Newtonsoft.Json;

namespace LooksFamiliar.Microservice.Store
{
    // entity class that represents the message you want to send
    public class Message
    {
        [JsonProperty(PropertyName = "id")]
        public string id { get; set; }
        public int cachettl { get; set; }
        public string sender { get; set; }
        public DateTime timestamp { get; set; }
        public string body { get; set; }
    }

    // the class that encapsulates a Service Bus Queue
    public class Queue
    {
        private static QueueClient _queueClient;

        public void Connect(string queueName)
        {
            // connect to the queue
            var namespaceManager = NamespaceManager.Create();
            var queueDesc = namespaceManager.GetQueue(queueName);
            _queueClient = QueueClient.Create(queueDesc.Path);
        }

        public string Read()
        {
            string messageBody = null;
            BrokeredMessage brokeredMessage = null;
            brokeredMessage = _queueClient.Receive(TimeSpan.
            FromSeconds(5));
```

53

```csharp
            if (brokeredMessage == null) return null;
            messageBody = brokeredMessage.GetBody<string>();
            brokeredMessage.Complete();
            return messageBody;
        }

        public void Write(string message)
        {
            var brokeredMessage = new BrokeredMessage(message)
            {
                MessageId = Guid.NewGuid().ToString()
            };
            _queueClient.Send(brokeredMessage);
        }
    }

    // class that queues a message
    public class Log
    {
        public void Message(string sender, string body)
        {
            var queue = new Queue();

            // connect to a queue named 'log'
            queue.Connect("log");

            // create a message and deserialize to json
            var message = new Message
            {
                id = Guid.NewGuid().ToString(),
                cachettl = 5,
                sender = sender,
                timestamp = DateTime.Now,
                body = body
            };

            var json = JsonConvert.SerializeObject(message);

            // send the message
            queue.Write(json);
        }
    }
}
```

API Management

API management provides API gateway services such as creating API proxies, configuring SSL and authentication, developer subscription key management, policy injection such as rate throttling or message transformations from JSON to XML or XML to JSON, and performance and health analytics.

The basic concept is that you place your API under management so that direct calls are never made by clients to your API. Incoming calls first arrive at the API proxy, policies are applied, and then the call is forwarded on. When the call returns to the API proxy, it applies any outgoing policies and the output is returned to the caller.

A developer key must be included in the API call in order for the call to pass through to the actual API. That means that anyone who wants to invoke your API must first register on the Developer Portal and request to subscribe to the API. Once they are approved, they receive a key. The developer key is the element that allows the service to gather statistics on who is calling, how often, and what performance those invocations are receiving.

Once you create an instance of API Management using the Azure Portal, both an Administrator Dashboard and a Developer Portal are provided (see Figures 4-18 and 4-19). The Administrator Dashboard provides the tools necessary to define API products and developer groups, and access the Analytics reports. Once a developer is registered on the Developer Portal, he or she will be able to gain access to API documentation and consoles for accessing sample code, making test calls, and examining return messages.

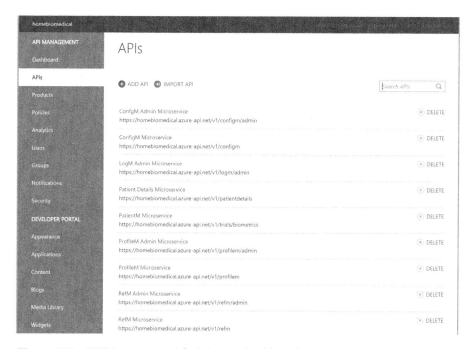

Figure 4-18. *API Management Administrator Dashboard*

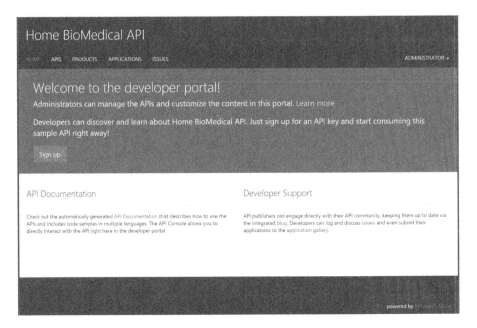

Figure 4-19. *API Management Developer Portal*

API Proxies

Using the Administrator Dashboard, you can define an API Proxy by providing the location of service you are registering and a new suffix that will be used to append to the API Management instance URL. For example, let's say the endpoint for your Reference Data API is hosted at `https://refmpublic.azurewebsites.net/ref`.

Once configured in an API Management instance called `myapi`, the new base URL would be `https://myapi.azure-api.net`.

You then define a suffix that is appended to the end of the base URL. A best practice is to use this proxy naming feature to add versioning to your APIs.

```
https://myapi.azure-api.net/v1/ref
```

You can also provide a friendly name and description producing documentation for the API (see Figure 4-20).

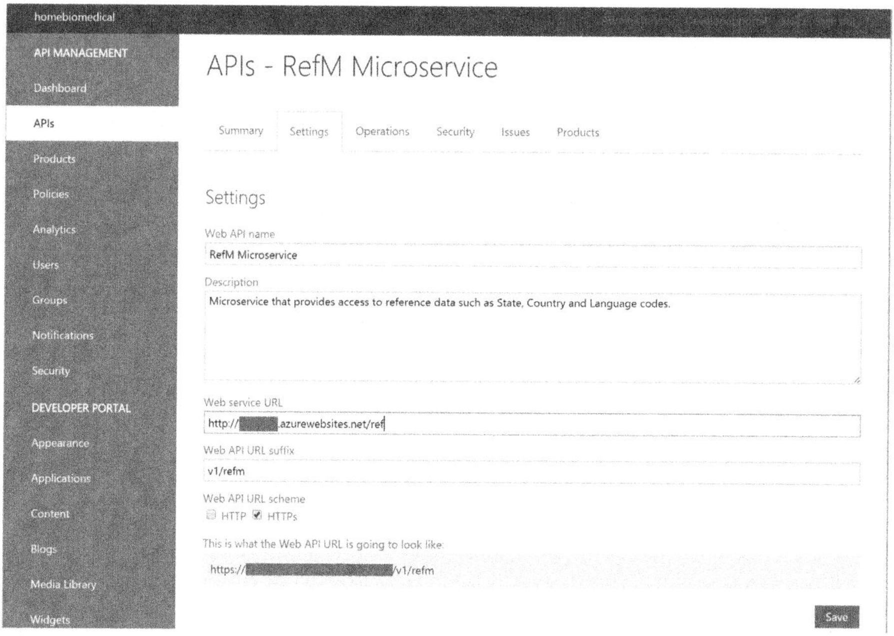

Figure 4-20. API Proxy Definition

Next, define the ReST operations exposed by the underlying API, adding documentation for each call and its parameters (see Figure 4-21 and Figure 4-22).

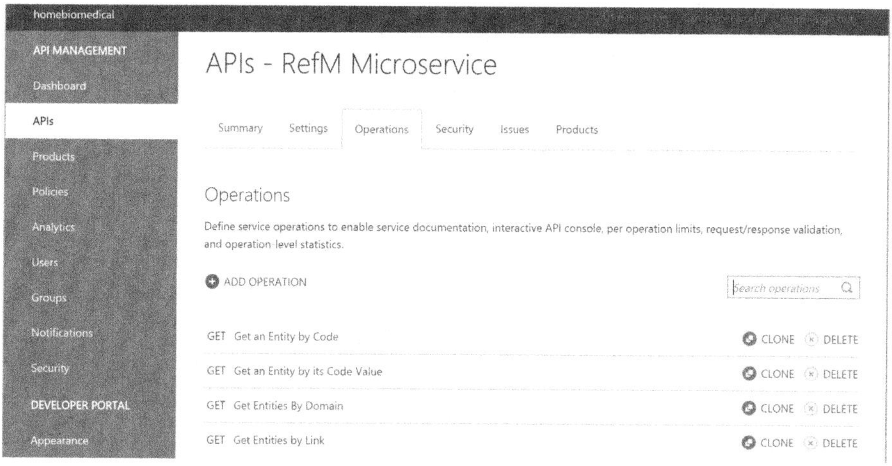

Figure 4-21. RefM API Operations

57

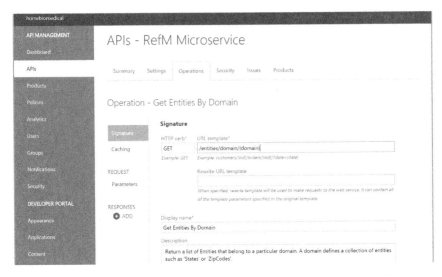

Figure 4-22. *RefM Get Entities by Domain API Operation Details*

API Subscriptions

The first time a developer visits the Developer Portal, they are presented with a login screen. Authentication to the Developer Portal can be done using a user name/password, Azure Active Directory credentials, or Microsoft, Facebook, Twitter, or Google accounts (see Figure 4-23).

Figure 4-23. *API Developer Portal Authentication*

Once authenticated, a developer will request access to APIs through API products. API products are collections of APIs with specific developer group access defined by the administrator (see Figure 4-24).

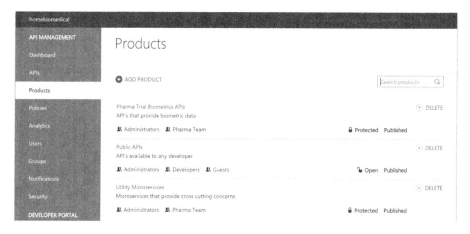

Figure 4-24. *API Products*

After a developer has successfully subscribed to an API product, their developer key will be generated and available for access on their profile page in the Developer Portal (see Figure 4-25).

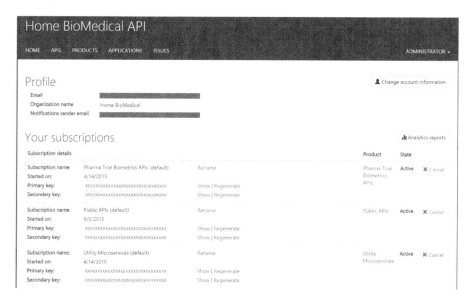

Figure 4-25. *Developer profile page for accessing developer keys*

59

The developer can visit the API page of the Developer Portal to access the API consoles. Each API has a generated console page that displays documentation created through the Administrators Dashboard, the location of the service endpoint and format of the parameters, code samples in several languages, and the ability to invoke the API (see Figure 4-26).

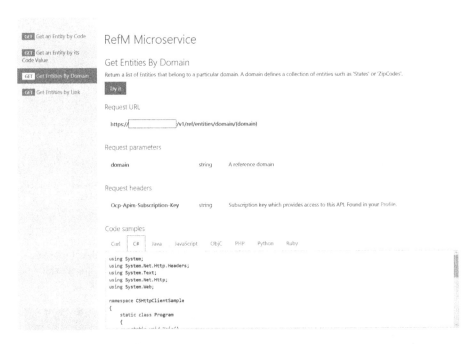

Figure 4-26. *API Console*

If the developer clicks the Try It button, they are presented a page where they can enter any parameters required by the API and then send the request. Upon return, they will see the response code, response time, and the message that was returned, usually either XML or JSON (see Figure 4-27).

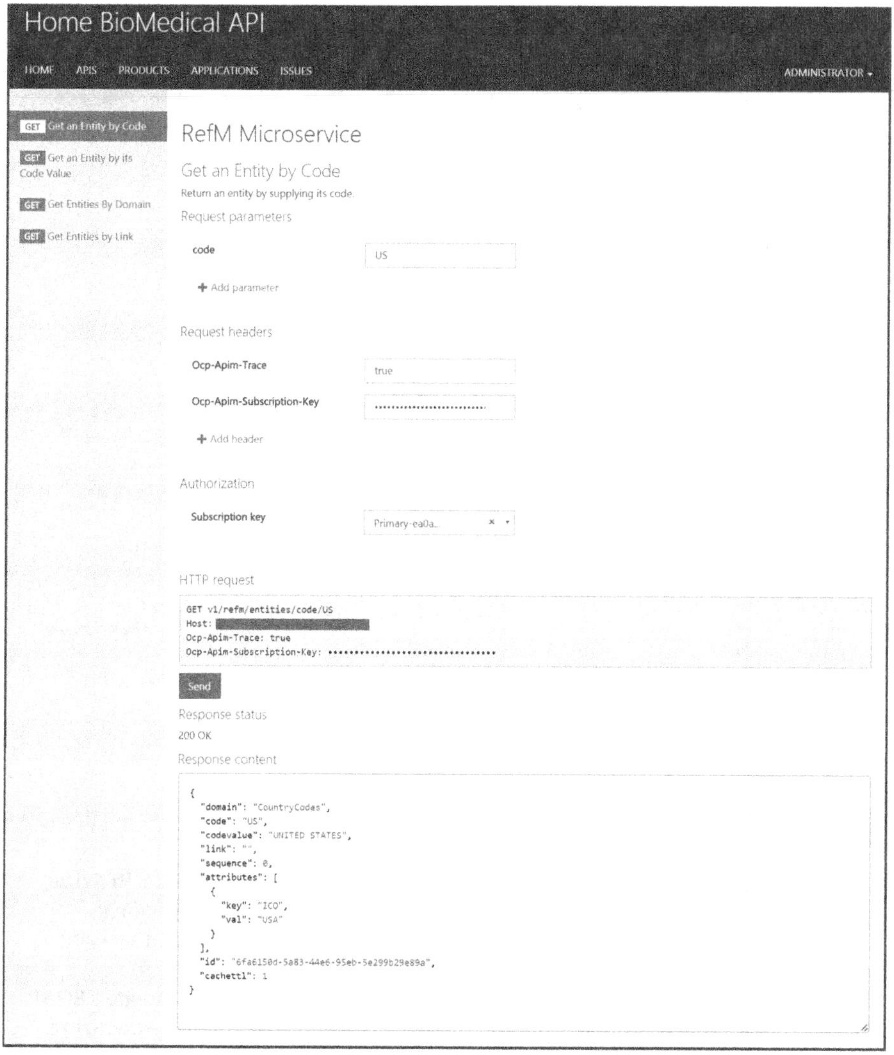

Figure 4-27. *API Console Try It Results*

Policy Injection

Policies allow you to set incoming and outgoing rules at the product, API, and operation levels. API Management provides a built-in library of injection policies covering cross-domain calls, authentication, JSON and XML conversion, rate limiting, usage quotas, rewriting URLs, and much more. The Policy Definition Editor allows you to inject polices into a configuration file, specifying them as input or output rules (see Figure 4-28).

Figure 4-28. *Policy Injection*

Containers

Containers are the environments in which you deploy and execute your code. In Azure, there are several choices for deploying and executing code. Deciding which one to use is usually driven by the technology stack chosen for implementation and security configuration considerations.

If you are leveraging Windows Communication Foundation (WCF) to create a SOAP or ReST API or a worker role that listens on a Service Bus queue, you will use the Azure Cloud Service container for deployment. If you are using ASP.NET Web API, you will use Azure App Services.

Cloud Services and App Services

There is an enormous amount of documentation on the development of Cloud Services and ASP.NET Web API so I will not cover those details here. Instead let's focus on the configuration aspects of these containers. Both Cloud Services and App Services allow you to configure elasticity.

Figure 4-29 shows an example of setting the elasticity rules for a Cloud Service worker role that is associated with a Service Bus queue. The minimum number of instances is set to 2 and the maximum is set to 5. The rule to bring another instance online is based on the number of messages in the queue.

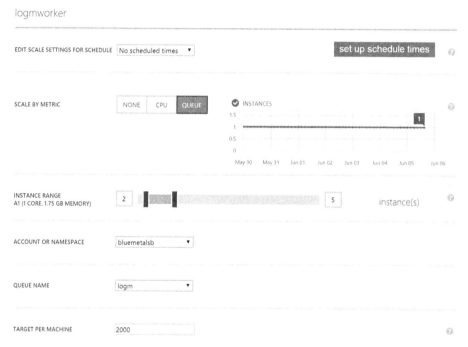

Figure 4-29. *Worker Role Elasticity Configuration*

In Figure 4-30, the App Service elasticity settings are based on the CPU and with separate settings for work day, work night, and weekends.

Figure 4-30. *App Service Elasticity Configuration*

Summary

This chapter provided a primer on several of the Azure finished services that provide the foundation for modern applications and microservices. Each service follows a predictable pattern of create, configure, and program using a language-specific SDK or going directly to the ReST APIs. As you move forward, you will be looking at custom microservices that follow this pattern of providing a programmable API and a management API, and that take advantage of the elastic containers that Azure provides. You will also look at how to automate provisioning, build, and deployment of Azure services and custom code.

The Reference Implementation that that you will use to perform this analysis is called The Home Biomedical Solution. It demonstrates how to implement, build, and deploy custom microservices that leverage DocumentDb, Redis Cache, SQL Database, and Service Bus. Each microservice provides both a public API and a management API, and provides client SDKs for invoking those APIs. Both Azure web sites and Cloud Services are demonstrated. Service Bus is used to provide high volume telemetry ingestion for Internet of Things devices as well as notification hubs for real-time mobile alerts. Stream Analytics is leverage for telemetry transformation and routing to storage as well as another Event Hub which is used to collect alarm events (see Figure 4-31).

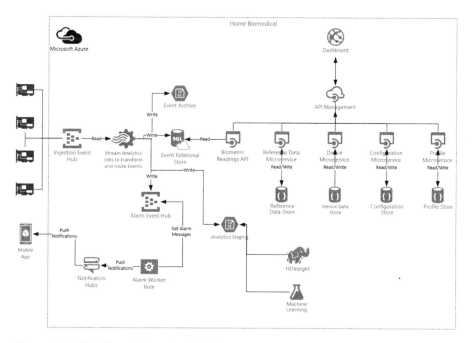

Figure 4-31. *The Home Biomedical Solution*

Before you dive into the code, though, it is important to understand how you can automate the provisioning, build, and deployment of this solution. As you have learned, Software as a Service is a business model that is built on the ability to automate the software product development process. In the next chapter, you will look at how to provision Azure services, build software assets, and deploy to Azure using PowerShell.

CHAPTER 5

▓ ▓ ▓

Automation

Automation is defined as the controlled operation of an apparatus, process, or system by mechanical or electronic devices that take the place of human labor. Automation is desirable because when we attempt to manually implement complex processes, we make mistakes, and these mistakes have a ripple effect that, many times, takes a vigorous root cause analysis to correct. Automation can seem like an expense when you are at the start of a project but investing in automation will pay dividends as systems grow and become more sophisticated. Common tasks become repeatable and measurable, and the code that implements these tasks is placed under source code control and is maintained in sync with the software and systems that are being automated. Automation synchronizes the infrastructure with the application code.

In order to realize the technical benefits of a microservice architecture and the business value of a Continuous Delivery Software as a Service solution, you will want to automate as much of the product development lifecycle as you can. There is no expectation that you will achieve 100% automation. Humans, whether we like it or not, are still involved in the process of providing oversight and quality assurance. It is, however, always possible that errors will be introduced. The goal is to minimize that effect by making automation a first-class citizen in the software development lifecycle.

DevOps is a term that is applied to the cultural approach to automation as well as one that describes the process and the tools. From a cultural perspective, DevOps promotes integration and collaboration of development and operations teams. The teams work together to design and develop the process and the tools that will automate the product development lifecycle. You will want to encourage cross-functional teams that combine architecture, development, testing, and operations. A cross-functional team will have all the skills necessary to carry the product development lifecycle from design through deployment.

Automation can be applied in the following four primary areas (also depicted in Figure 5-1):

- **Provisioning**: Provisioning involves planning the cloud resources that will be required, manually creating the resources, documenting the initial configurations, and creating the automation scripts that will be used to create the cloud environment on demand.

- **Build/Test**: Building software and automated testing has been around for some time now. Continuous Integration is the practice of using software tools to merge code updates, compile and integrate software assets, and run automated unit tests.

- **Deployment**: Deployment automates the packaging of the software assets and data, deploying them to a staging environment for acceptance testing, and then automating the move from staging to production.

- **Management**: Management is the automation of the cloud resource configuration, providing control over scale up, scale down, spin up, spin down, sizing, monitoring, and lifetime.

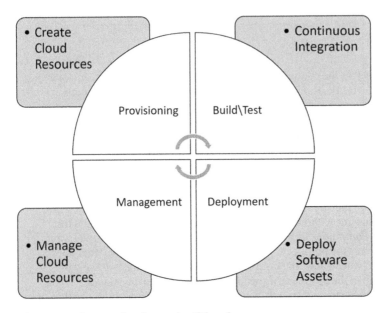

Figure 5-1. *Automating the product lifecycle*

There are many tools and technologies that you can leverage to provide automation in each of these areas. PowerShell has emerged as the primary tool for automating provisioning and deployment for Azure. In addition, you can leverage Azure Resource Manager templates, Azure's ReST API, and .NET Client SDKs to perform various provisioning and deployment tasks. There are also third-party tools such as Puppet and Chef that have emerged as enterprise class products that support product lifecycle automation.

The goal of this chapter is to introduce you to the process of automating Azure. You will use scripts provided as part of the Home Biomedical Reference Implementation to provision, build, and deploy of the solution. You will do the following:

- Use PowerShell to provision the shared resources DocumentDb, Redis Cache, and Azure Storage.

- Use PowerShell and C# to provision isolated runtime environments for each of the microservices that make up the reference implementation.

- Use PowerShell to build the software assets that define the solution.

- Use PowerShell and C# to deploy data and software assets to Azure.

- Use a combination of management consoles, Postman, and SQL Server Management Studio to validate the deployment.

Azure PowerShell

Azure PowerShell is installed using the Microsoft Web Platform Installer. The Web Installer installs the Azure PowerShell cmdlets and their dependencies. Azure cmdlets are PowerShell modules that automate Azure tasks. Once installed, you can get to the PowerShell console by typing 'power' from the start screen.

Microsoft Web Platform Installer
http://go.microsoft.com/fwlink/p/?linkid=320376&clcid=0x409

Next, you want to connect to your subscription. If you don't have a subscription, you can visit http://azure.net and follow the instructions to set up a trial subscription.

Get Started with Azure
http://go.microsoft.com/fwlink/p/?linkid=320795&clcid=0x409

Before you begin, you want to make sure you have the rights to execute scripts in your environment. Use the Set-ExecutionPolicy command to configure the execution policy. Run the PowerShell console with administrative rights and execute this command:

```
> Set-ExecutionPolicy
    -ExecutionPolicy Unrestricted
    -Scope CurrentUser
    -Force
```

At the console, type the following command to add your subscription. You will be prompted to enter your Azure account credentials.

```
> Add-AzureAccount
```

You can configure multiple Azure accounts and subscriptions. To see a list of the available accounts and subscriptions, you can use these commands:

```
> Get-AzureAccount
> Get-AzureSubscription
```

To select a specific Azure subscription, use this command:

```
> Select-AzureSubscription  <subscription-name>
```

To get help, you can type the following commands to get various levels of assistance:

```
> Get-Help
> Get-Help Azure
> Get-Help <azure-cmdlet-name>
> Get-Help <azure-cmdlet-name> -examples
> Get-Help <azure-cmdlet-name> -full
```

PowerShell Consoles

There are two applications that you will find most useful: the Windows PowerShell ISE (see Figure 5-2) and the Windows PowerShell console. The PowerShell ISE provides an editor with multiple tabs and line numbers as well as a console where you can type in commands directly. When developing scripts, you can run the entire script or highlight a portion and execute only that section.

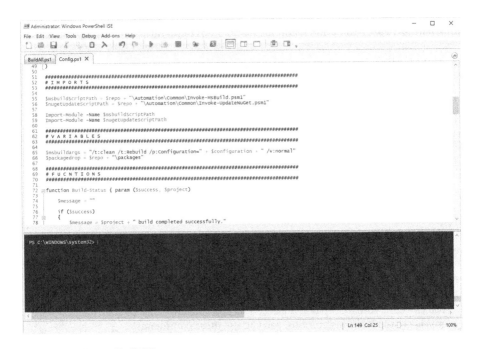

Figure 5-2. *PowerShell ISE*

The PowerShell console is a command line utility that you can use to type in PowerShell commands directly and to run scripts. It is recommended that you run both of these applications with administrator privileges.

Provisioning

The first step in automating the provisioning process is to build the environment manually using the Azure Management Console and the Preview portal (see Figure 5-3).

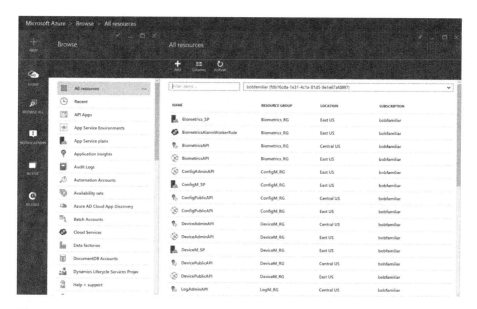

Figure 5-3. *Azure Preview Portal*

▪ **Note**   At the time of this writing, you will need to use both the Classic console and the Preview portal because some resources are managed in the Classic portal and others in the Preview portal.

The creation of resources by hand is typically done at the start of the project as the architecture emerges from initial minimum viable product development efforts. When the environment has reached a point of minimal functionality, you examine what has been manually instantiated and document the configuration settings. Using Azure PowerShell cmdlets, you then script the creation of each cloud resource. In order to provide organization across all the autonomous, independently deployed services, Azure provides a construct called Azure resource groups.

Azure Resource Groups

Azure resource groups are useful logical constructs into which you provision resources and deploy software. Resource groups provide lifecycle boundaries. You can use resource groups to collect and manage a set of application resources such as all the various components of a microservice. The Azure Preview portal allows you to view, monitor, and track your usage and billing for all the resources within a resource group (see Figure 5-4).

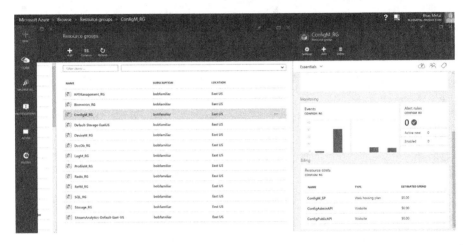

Figure 5-4. *Azure Resource Groups*

You can manually create Azure resources within Azure resource groups by first selecting the group in the Preview portal and then clicking the Add button. A list of resources is displayed (see Figure 5-5).

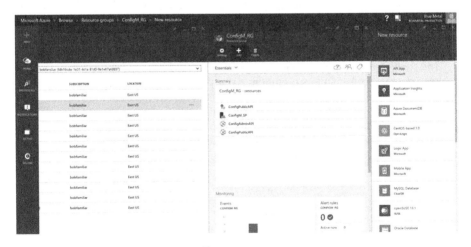

Figure 5-5. *Adding a resource manually to a resource group*

As part of preparing the environment for the Home Biomedical Reference Implementation, you will automate the creation of several resource groups, one for each microservice that makes up the solution. By defining resources within specific resource groups, you will have control over the lifetime of those resources as a single entity. This approach fulfills the "isolation" and "autonomous" requirements of the microservices approach.

The Home Biomedical Git Repository

The code repository for the Home Biomedical Reference Implementation is available online. As we move through the various scripts and solutions, I will refer to code and scripts located within this repository.

■ **Note**   The repository is located at https://microservices.codeplex.com/.

The Git repository can be cloned using this command:

git clone https://git01.codeplex.com/microservices

The reference implementation was developed using Visual Studio 2015, .NET 4.5.2, Azure SDK for .NET 2.7.1, and Azure PowerShell 0.9.8. Refer to the ReadMe for additional details on the development environment requirements.

At the root of the repository are common automation scripts, sample client applications, utilities, and a folder containing NuGet packages for each of the assemblies that make up the microservices. The source code, projects, and solutions for the microservices are organized into a set of hierarchical folders underneath the Microservices folder. The structure of the repository is depicted in Figure 5-6.

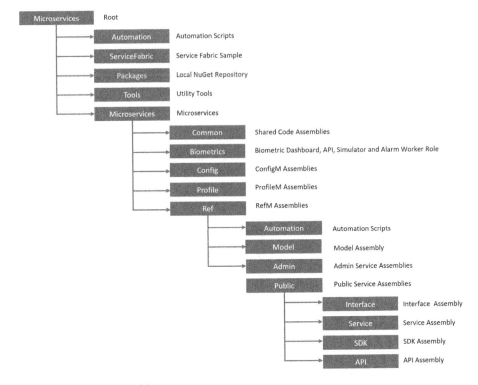

Figure 5-6. Git Repo Folder Structure

The namespaces for the reference implementation also follow this folder format. For example, the namespace definitions for the Config microservice are as follows:

```
LooksFamiliar.Microservices.Config.Models
LooksFamiliar.Microservices.Config.Admin.Interface
LooksFamiliar.Microservices.Config.Admin.Service
LooksFamiliar.Microservices.Config.Admin.SDK
LooksFamiliar.Microservices.Config.Public.Interface
LooksFamiliar.Microservices.Config.Public.Service
LooksFamiliar.Microservices.Config.Public.SDK
```

The source code for each component assembly is found in its own Visual Studio solution. There is no monolithic solution that combines all the projects; this may be different from how you usually work. I have instead deconstructed the code organization to further emphasize the architecture. I leveraged NuGet as a means to manage assembly references. I used PowerShell automation scripts to pull everything together for build, test, and deploy.

Your approach to how you organize and manage source code, solutions, and projects will very likely differ. The point of this book is not to promote a single approach, but instead to outline a pattern. How you choose to realize that pattern is left to your creativity.

Provisioning Azure Resources

To provision Azure resources, you create PowerShell scripts that leverage the Azure cmdlets. Each step of the provisioning process should have its own script to perform a particular task, such as the creation of an Azure storage account or an Azure resource group. Each script should take as input the set of parameters it requires so as to make the script as reusable as possible. For example, the Create-ResourceGroup.Ps1 script takes three parameters:

- Subscription: The name of your Azure subscription

- ResourceGroupName: The name of the resource group to create

- AzureLocation: The region in which you want to create the resource group, such as East US, West US, East US 2, etc.

The script uses CmdletBinding to define the input parameters:

```
[CmdletBinding()]
Param
(
    [Parameter(Mandatory=$True,
               Position=0,
               HelpMessage="The subscription name.")]
    [string]$Subscription,
    [Parameter(Mandatory=$True,
               Position=1,
               HelpMessage="The resource group name.")]
    [string]$ResourceGroupName,
    [Parameter(Mandatory=$True,
               Position=2,
               HelpMessage="The name of the Azure Region")]
    [string]$AzureLocation
)
```

The script executes two Azure PowerShell commands to select a subscription and create a resource group:

```
> Select-Subscription $Subscription
> New-AzureResourceGroup
    -Name $ResourceGroupName
    -Location $AzureLocation
```

When you run this script using the PowerShell console, you are prompted to enter each parameter. The script outputs the status at each step so you can track its progress (see Figure 5-7).

```
PS C:\Users\bobfa\source\repos\looksfamiliar\automation\provision\scripts> .\Create-ResourceGroup

cmdlet Create-ResourceGroup.ps1 at command pipeline position 1
Supply values for the following parameters:
(Type !? for Help.)
Subscription: bobfamiliar_test
ResourceGroupName: Test_RG
AzureLocation: East US


SubscriptionId         :
SubscriptionName       : bobfamiliar_test
Environment            : AzureCloud
SupportedModes         : AzureServiceManagement,AzureResourceManager
DefaultAccount         :
Accounts               :
IsDefault              : True
IsCurrent              : True
CurrentStorageAccountName :
TenantId               :

VERBOSE: 9:46:42 AM - Created resource group 'Test_RG' in location 'eastus'
ResourceGroupName : Test_RG
Location          : eastus
Resources         : {}
ResourcesTable    :
ProvisioningState : Succeeded
Permissions       : {Microsoft.Azure.Commands.Resources.Models.Authorization.PSPermission}
PermissionsTable  :
                    Actions  NotActions
                    =======  ==========
                    *

Tags              : {}
TagsTable         :
ResourceId        : /subscriptions/77d19f95-8966-4b89-87a1-beb03450dd60/resourceGroups/Test_RG

VERBOSE: Elapse Time (Seconds): 6.9797091

PS C:\Users\bobfa\source\repos\looksfamiliar\automation\provision\scripts>
```

Figure 5-7. *Create-ResourceGroup Script Execution*

■ **Note**   You can try this out by starting the PowerShell console and navigating to the automation\common folder in the repository. Type the following commands and follow the script prompts:

```
> add-azureaccount
> switch-azuremode AzureResourceManager
> .\create-resourcegroup
```

Console Application Integration

You may discover that some steps in the automation process are best implemented using code. There are a couple of approaches when using code to implement an automation task. You can create PowerShell cmdlets in C# and then integrate those assemblies into your environment using the Import-Module command. Another approach is to create a console application and then wrap the call to the console application in a PowerShell script that invokes an executable. For the Home Biomedical Reference Implementation, I have opted to use the later approach. An example of this can be found in the code that provisions Service Bus Event Hubs.

The SBUpdate console application takes as input the Service Bus connection string and the name of the Event Hub to be created. It uses the NamespaceManager client to create the Event Hub.

```
var client = NamespaceManager.CreateFromConnectionString(
    ConnectionString);
client.CreateEventHub(EventHubName);
```

▦ **Note**   To review the code that implements this console application, see tools\SBUpdate\SBUpdate.sln.

You can call a console application from PowerShell using the & symbol followed by the path to the executable. You can encapsulate that call and provide support for the command line arguments by creating a PowerShell module. A PowerShell module defines and exports a PowerShell function. An example of this can be found in the Create-EventHub.psm1 module.

```
function Create-EventHub
{
  param ($Repo, $ConnStr, $EventHubName)

  $sbupdate = $Repo + "\Automation\Tools\sbupdate\SBUpdate.exe"
  $sbparams = "-connstr", $ConnStr, "-eventhub", $EventHubName
  & $sbupdate $sbparams
}
Export-ModuleMember -Function Create-EventHub
```

To invoke this module in another script, use the Import-Module command to reference the module file. You can see an example of this in the Create-ServiceBus.ps1 script.

```
$CreateEH = $Repo + "\Automation\Common\Create-EventHub.psm1"
Import-Module -Name $CreateEH
```

Once imported, the function can be called directly in the script, like so:
```
Create-EventHub $Repo $ConnStr $EHBiometrics
```

▦ **Note**   There are several PowerShell modules used by the Reference Implementation's automation scripts. You will find them in automation\common.

The console application executables are found in automation\tools and the source code for those tools can be found in the top-level Tools folder in the repo (repository).

If you modify one of the console utilities, drop the new executable into the appropriate folder in automation\tools.

Provisioning Shared Services

The first step in the provisioning process is to build out the shared services that will be used by the microservices. These include Storage, DocumentDb, and Redis Cache. The provisioning script to set up these common services is located in \automation\provision and is called Provision.ps1. The script takes five parameters:

- Repo: The path to the Git repo on your machine

- Subscription: The name of your Azure subscription

- AzureLocation: The name of the region you are deploying to, such as East US, East US 2, West US, etc.

- Prefix: A value that will appended to the front of the core name of the Azure resources to make them unique

- Suffix: A value that will specify if the deployment is dev, test, or prod.

The Prefix is necessary as many Azure resources need to have a unique name within the Azure global namespace. The Prefix will be appended to a base name that is defined in the Provision script and the Suffix will be added to the end. This combination should make the resources unique within Azure as well as within your environments.

EXERCISE 1

The first exercise is to provision the shared resources for the Home Biomedical Reference Implementation.

1. Navigate to the \automation\provision folder. If you have not yet added your Azure account information, type

   ```
   > add-azureaccount
   ```

2. Enter your credentials to initialize your environment. To run the shared services provisioning script, type

   ```
   > .\provision
   ```

You will be promoted for the input arguments. When complete, you should see a list of Azure resources that look something like what is depicted in Figure 5-8.

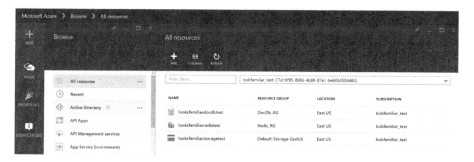

Figure 5-8. *Azure environment after provisioning shared resources*

Collecting Connection Strings

In order to deploy data to DocumentDb and for the microservices to connect to DocumentDb and Redis Cache, the connections strings for both need to be collected from the portal. A file called `Include-ConnectionStrings.ps1` is located in the automation folder off the root of the Git repo. Open this file for editing and follow the directions below to collect the connection strings and place them in this file. The settings you are looking for are the DocumentDb URL, the DocumentDb Key, the DocumentDb Connection String, and the Redis URL.

EXERCISE 2

In this exercise, you will gather the connections strings for DocumentDb and Redis Cache and place them in a common script file.

1. Using the Preview portal, navigate to your DocumentDb instance and select Settings ➤ Keys. The Keys blade will appear (see Figure 5-9).

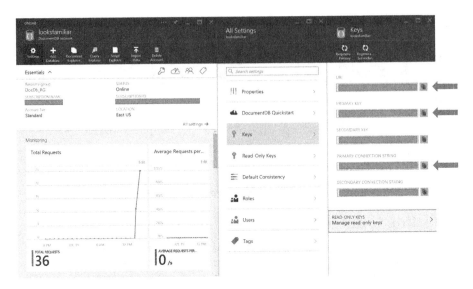

Figure 5-9. *DocumentDb Keys Blade*

2. Copy the URI, Primary Key, and Primary Connection String values and paste them into the Include-ConnectionStrings.ps1 file.

```
$docdbconnstr = "<docdb-connection-string>"
$docdburi = "<docdb-uri>"
$docdbkey = "<docdb-key>"
```

3. Navigate to the Redis Cache Settings blade. The Redis URI is constructed using two values from the Redis settings page, the host name and the primary key (see Figure 5-10).

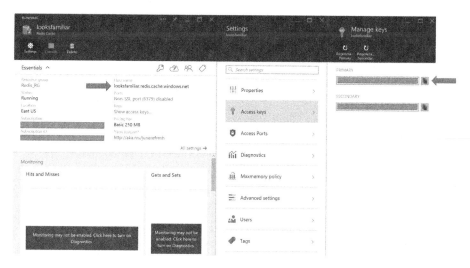

Figure 5-10. *Redis Keys*

4. Copy the host name and primary key values from the Redis Cache blade and put them together to form the Redis URL using the following format in the `Include-ConnectionStrings.ps1`:

   ```
   $redisuri = "<hostname>,ssl=true,password=<primary-key>"
   ```

Provisioning Microservices

Now that the shared services are provisioned, you can move onto the microservices themselves. There are four microservices that provide the cross-cutting and business capabilities for your solution.

- **ConfigM** provides discoverability and configuration services.
- **RefM** provides reference data services.
- **ProfileM** provides user profile services.
- **DeviceM** provides device registration and provisioning services.

Each microservice has its own `automation` folder with four scripts. For example, if you navigate to the `microservices\ref\automation` folder you will see the files shown in Figure 5-11.

81

Name	Date modified	Type
01-Provision-RefM.ps1	9/2/2015 3:29 PM	Windows PowerShell Script
02-Build-RefM.ps1	8/28/2015 12:56 PM	Windows PowerShell Script
03-Deploy-RefM.ps1	9/4/2015 11:01 AM	Windows PowerShell Script
Package-RefM.ps1	8/28/2015 12:56 PM	Windows PowerShell Script

Figure 5-11. *RefM Microservice Automation Scripts*

The scripts in the microservice `automation` folders have been numbered to emphasize the order in which they are run. Here is a description of each script:

- `01-Provision-[Microservice Name].ps1`: This script provisions the resources needed for this microservice.

- `02-Build-[Microservice Name].ps1`: This script automates the build of all the microservice assemblies, NuGet packages, and deployable solutions.

- `03-Deploy-[Microservice Name].ps1`: This script deploys data, packages, and publishes the microservice solutions.

- `Package-[Microservice Name].ps1`: This script is used by the Deploy script to package the microservice in preparation for deployment to Azure. You do not run this script directly.

Just like the shared services provisioning script, the individual microservice provisioning scripts take the same five parameters: `Repo`, `Subscription`, `AzureLocation`, `Prefix`, and `Suffix` (see Figure 5-12).

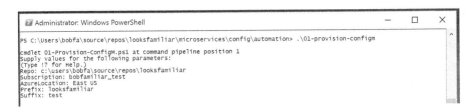

Figure 5-12. *Invoking the ConfigM provisioning script*

EXERCISE 3

In this exercise, you will provision each of the microservices in the Home Biomedical Reference Implementation.

1. Navigate to the `\microservices\config\automation` folder.

2. Type the following at the command prompt:

   ```
   > .\provision-configm
   ```

3. Enter the parameters when prompted.

   When it is complete, the ConfigM resource group will be created and will contain an App Service Plan and two Azure website containers, as shown in Figure 5-13.

Figure 5-13. *State of Azure after ConfigM provisioning*

If you examine the ConfigM provisioning script, you will see that it is leveraging scripts in the `Automation\Common` folder to create a resource group and then creating an application service and two Azure website containers in that resource group.

```
# Create Resource Group
.\..\..\..\Automation\Common\Create-ResourceGroup.ps1
  $Subscription $ConfigM_RG $AzureLocation

# create app service plans
.\..\..\..\Automation\Common\Create-AppServicePlan
  $Subscription $ConfigM_RG $ConfigM_SP $AzureLocation
```

```
# create web site containers
.\..\..\..\Automation\Common\Create-WebSite.ps1 $Subscription
  $ConfigAdminAPI  $ConfigM_RG $ConfigM_SP $AzureLocation
.\..\..\..\Automation\Common\Create-WebSite.ps1 $Subscription
  $ConfigPublicAPI $ConfigM_RG $ConfigM_SP $AzureLocation
```

Because these resources all exist in the same resource group, it is very straightforward to deprovision them with a single command, like so:

```
> remove-azureresourcegroup -Name $ConfigM_RG -force –Verbose
```

Repeat the provioning step for the remaining three microservices (RefM, ProfileM, and DeviceM).

4. Navigate to the `microservices\device\automation` folder and execute `01-provision-devicem.ps1`.

5. Navigate to the `microservices\profile\automation` folder and execute `01-provision-profilem.ps1`.

6. Navigate to the `microservices\ref\automation` folder and execute `01-provision-refm.ps1`.

Provisioning the Biometrics Microservice

Biometrics is a microservice that consists of Service Bus Event Hubs, Notification Hubs, Stream Analytics jobs, and a SQL Database along with a custom cloud service for handling alarm conditions, an API over the SQL Database, and a data visualization website that leverages SignalR to invoke the API. All together they provide the IoT capabilities of the Home Biomedical solution. Therefore, the Biometrics provisioning script performs some additional steps.

In addition to the resource groups, service plans, and website containers for the API and website, the provisioning script will create the following:

- A Cloud Service container for hosting the Alarm Notification service

- A Service Bus namespace, two Event Hubs called biometrics and alarms, and a Notification Hub called alarms

- Five Stream Analytics jobs that will stream and transform incoming telemetry from the biometrics Event Hub and redirect to SQL Database or in the case of alarms, to the Alarm Event Hub

- A SQL Database instance with a database called `BiometricsDb` that will be used to capture the real-time biometric telemetry

EXERCISE 4

In this exercise, you will provision the Biometrics microservice resources.

1. Navigate to the `microservices\biometrics\automation` and run the provisioning script, providing the same five input arguments as before:

   ```
   > .\01-provision-biometrics
   ```

When you are finished provisioning, your Azure environment should look similar to what is depicted in Figure 5-14.

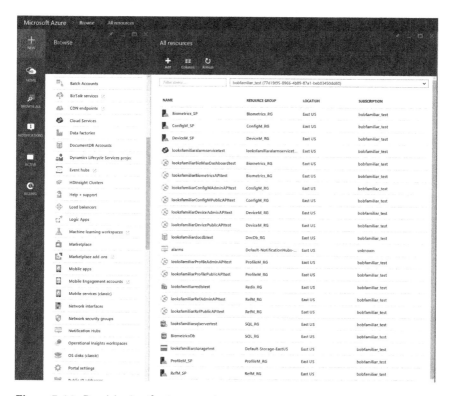

Figure 5-14. *Provisioning the Azure environment*

The provisioning scripts have prepared your Azure subscription environment for the eventual deployment of the microservices and the Biometrics subsystem, but before you can deploy, you must build.

Build

The Home Biomedical Reference Implementation provides a set of build scripts that demonstrate the use of PowerShell to automate a build process in order to prepare the software assets for deployment. Each solution is built in a specific order to update dependencies dynamically. The software provided makes heavy use of NuGet packages with versioning. The build automation provides the mechanism to make sure all the software assets reference the latest version of each NuGet package.

NuGet Packaging

When dealing with many solutions that are referencing common assemblies, it can become burdensome to manage all the assembly references. NuGet provides a mechanism to create versioned packages for your assemblies that you can use within the context of your development team or, if you so choose to, share with the developer community online.

All of the supporting assemblies that make up the microservices are built as NuGet packages and dropped into the Packages folder off the root of the Git repo. Each microservice is constructed out of a set of assemblies that follow a consistent naming pattern. Each of those assemblies follows a consistent referencing pattern, depicted in Figure 5-15. Each microservice follows this pattern, so if you understand one, you understand them all.

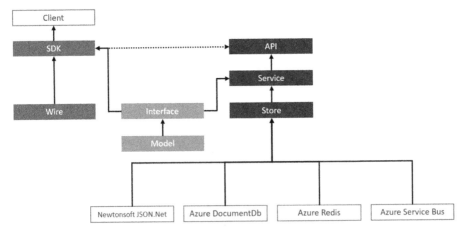

Figure 5-15. NuGet Package Reference Model

- A Client application references the SDK NuGet package, which provides a proxy class for calling the microservice API.

- The microservice API provides the protocol implementation and references the Service NuGet package.

- The SDK and the Service reference common Interface and Model NuGet packages, providing harmony between client and server.

- The SDK references the Wire NuGet package to make ReST calls.

- The Service references the Store NuGet package for persistence.

- The Store assembly references the Azure SDKs for DocumentDb, Redis Cache, and Service Bus.

To successfully build the Reference Implementation, you will need to modify the NuGet Package Manager settings in Visual Studio to reference the local NuGet package folder in the Git repo. Follow this menu path in Visual Studio: Tools Menu ➤ NuGet Package Manager ➤ Manage NuGet Packages for this solution. The NuGet Package Manager will display (see Figure 5-16).

Figure 5-16. *NuGet Package Manager*

Click the Options button ⚙ in the upper right corner of the manager window to bring up the options dialog (see Figure 5-17).

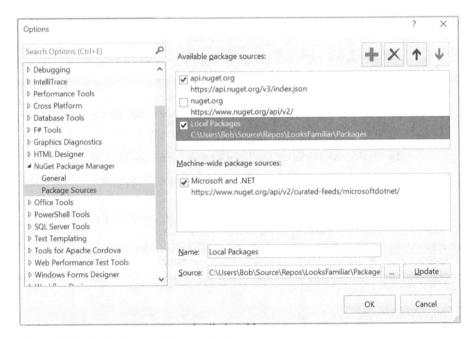

Figure 5-17. *NuGet Package Manager Options*

To add the NuGet Packages location for this repo, click the + icon to add an additional package location. Change the name to something meaningful (Local Packages, for example). Use the ... button to navigate to the Packages folder at the top level of the repo. Select the folder, click Update, and then OK. Now you can switch between the online NuGet catalogs and this local NuGet catalog when making NuGet package references. Referencing shared NuGet packages is now fully integrated into your development environment.

■ **Note** For more information on creating and publishing NuGet Packages, visit http://docs.nuget.org/create/creating-and-publishing-a-package.

Build Scripts

There are two common modules that are used by all the build scripts:

- **Invoke-MsBuild.psm1**: A PowerShell module to make building projects with MsBuild. It provides many features like fire-and-forget, or build-and-wait to check if build succeeded. This module was created by Daniel Schroeder and is available on CodePlex at https://invokemsbuild.codeplex.com/.

- **Invoke-UpdateNuGet.psm1**: A PowerShell module that encapsulates the call to the NuGetUpdate console application that updates local NuGet package references.

The NuGetUpdate console application makes sure that a solution references the latest version of the NuGet package by updating the packages.config XML file, deleting the associated assembly folder from the packages folder, and updating the .csproj XML file's ItemGroup section that references the assembly by version number.

▨ **Note**   To review the code that implements this utility, see
tools\NuGetUpdate\NuGetUpdate.sln.

EXERCISE 5

In this exercise, you will build the shared libraries and each of the microservices. There are two common assemblies used by all the microservices called Wire and Store.

1. To build the shared assemblies, navigate to microservices\common\automation and run the build scripts for Wire and Store. You will be promoted for two parameters: the path to the top level folder of the Git repo and the build configuration, debug, or release.

   > .\01-build-wire

   > .\02-build-store

2. To build the ConfigM microservice, navigate to the microservices\config\automation folder and type this command:

   > .\02-build-configm

Each assembly is built, and a new version of its NuGet package is dropped into the Packages folder off the root of the repo (see Figure 5-18). This automated build process makes sure that the dependencies across all assemblies are synchronized.

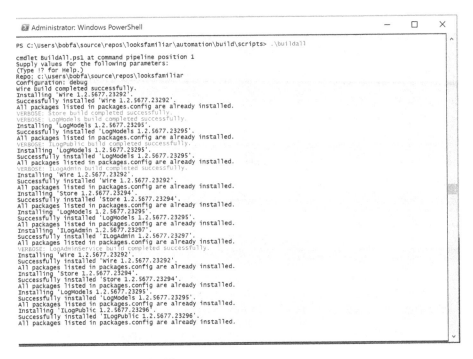

Figure 5-18. Running the build script

Repeat the build process for each of the remaining microservices (DeviceM, ProfileM, RefM, and Biometrics).

1. Navigate to the `microservices\device\automation` folder and execute the `02-build-devicem` script.

2. Navigate to the `microservices\profile\automation` folder and execute the `02-build-profilem` script.

3. Navigate to the `microservices\ref\automation` folder and execute the `02-build-refm` script.

4. Navigate to the `microservices\biometrics\automation` folder and execute the `02-build-biometrics` script.

Deployment

Once you have provisioned the Azure resources and successfully built the software, you are ready for deployment. The deployment scripts for the ConfigM, DeviceM, ProfileM, and RefM microservices perform these operations:

1. If requested, deploy data to DocumentDb.

2. Package the software for deployment.

3. Deploy the software.

The microservice deployment scripts take the same five parameters as the provisioning scripts. It is key that you use the same values you entered for provisioning to keep the deployments in sync with the provisioning. In addition to these five parameters, the microservices deployment scripts take an additional optional parameter called -DeployData.

Deploy Data

The deployment of the data is optional, since you may not want to do that every time. The deployment scripts utilize a PowerShell feature called a Switch parameter.

```
[switch]$DeployData
```

If the parameter is present (i.e. -DeployData is present on the command line), the value will be true. If it is not present, the value will be false. It is also possible to pass the value on the command as follows:

```
-DeployData:$true
```

or

```
-DeployData:$false
```

To run this command and have it load DocumentDb with the sample data, add the -DeployData parameter on the command line as follows:

```
> .\03-deploy-configm -DeployData:$true
```

The script evaluates this parameter, and if true, invokes the Load-DocDb.ps1 script. This script imports a module that invokes the DocumentDB Data Migration Tool utility. The DocumentDB Data Migration Tool is an open source solution to import data to DocumentDB from a variety of sources including JSON files, MongoDB, SQL Server, CSV files, Azure Table storage, and DocumentDB collections.

```
Load-DocDb.ps1
    -Repo $Repo
    -Subscription $Subscription
    -DocDbConnStr $connStr
    -CollectionName ManifestCollection
```

■ **Note**   You can download the latest version of the DocumentDb Data Migration Tool from www.microsoft.com/en-us/download/details.aspx?id=46436.

The data that will be used to initialize DocumentDb has been staged in automation\deploy\data. The data is in the form of JSON documents. Each JSON document represents a deserialized model for its associated microservice. They are used to initialize the ConfigM, ProfileM, RefM and DeviceM DocumentDb databases.

■ **Note**   There are console apps that can be used to regenerate the same JSON data if necessary. The data generation utilities are located in the tools\DbInit folder.

Generate Packages

Once the data is deployed, the next step in the script is to package the solution in preparation for deployment. In the case of an Azure website, MSBuild generates a ZIP file and associated files that define the application manifest (see Figure 5-19).

Name	Date modified	Type	Size
ConfigAdminAPI.deploy.cmd	9/5/2015 7:47 PM	Windows Command Script	15 KB
ConfigAdminAPI.deploy-readme.txt	9/5/2015 7:47 PM	Text Document	4 KB
ConfigAdminAPI.SetParameters.xml	9/5/2015 7:47 PM	XML File	1 KB
ConfigAdminAPI.SourceManifest.xml	9/5/2015 7:47 PM	XML File	1 KB
ConfigAdminAPI.zip	9/5/2015 7:47 PM	Compressed (zipped) Folder	5,511 KB

Figure 5-19. *Azure Website Package Files*

For Cloud Services, the MSBuild packaging process creates two files, a CSCFG (configuration) file and a .CSPKG (package) file (see Figure 5-20).

Name	Date modified	Type	Size
Extensions	9/4/2015 9:59 AM	File folder	
AlarmsWorker.cspkg	9/6/2015 9:25 AM	Service Package file	4,815 KB
ServiceConfiguration.Cloud.cscfg	9/6/2015 9:56 AM	Cloud Service Configuration file	2 KB

Figure 5-20. *Azure Cloud Service Package Files*

The MSBuild command line parameters to generate the package files for an Azure website are

```
MSbuild /t:Package /P:PackageLocation=<drop-path>
```

The MSBuild command line parameters to generate the package files for an Azure Cloud Service are

```
MSbuild /t:Publish /p:PublishDir=<drop-path>
```

The deployment scripts drop the packages into the automation\deploy\packages folder, where they are picked up by the next step in the process, which is to deploy to Azure.

Deploy Packages

The next step in the script is to take the packages and deploy them to the appropriate containers in Azure. The automation\common\Publish-WebSite.ps1 script is invoked to perform the operation. First, that script uploads the package files to blob storage.

```
$containerName = 'msdeploypackages'
$blobName = (Get-Date -Format 'ssmmhhddMMyyyy') + '-'
    + $ResourceGroupName + '-' + $DeploymentName
    + '-WebDeployPackage.zip'

if (!(Get-AzureStorageContainer
    $containerName -ErrorAction SilentlyContinue))
{
    New-AzureStorageContainer
        -Name $containerName
        -Permission Off
}

Set-AzureStorageBlobContent
    -Blob $blobName
    -Container $containerName
    -File $WebDeployPackage

# Create a SAS token, add it to the blob's URI
$webDeployPackageUri = New-AzureStorageBlobSASToken
    -Container $containerName
    -Blob $blobName
    -Permission r
    -FullUri
```

> ■ **Note** Shared access signatures (SAS tokens) allow secure, granular access to tables, queues, blob containers, and blobs. A SAS token can be configured to provide specific access rights, such as read, write, update, delete to a specific table, key range within a table, queue, blob, or blob container and do that for a specified time period or without any limit.

Next, the script generates a JSON file that contains the necessary input parameters and calls New-AzureResourceGroup. This command will create a new resource group if it does not exist or use the existing one. It will then deploy the package referenced in the generated JSON parameter file.

```
# generate the paramteres file for New-AzureResourceGroup
$ParametersFile = $Repo +
    "\Automation\Deploy\Scripts\Templates\" +
    $SiteName +
    ".json"
$JSON = @"
{
    "parameterValues": {
        "siteName": "$SiteName",
        "hostingPlanName": "$ServicePlan",
        "siteLocation": "$Location",
        "msdeployPackageUri":"$WebDeployPackageUri"
    }
}
"@
$JSON | Set-Content -Path $ParametersFile

# Read the values from the parameters file, create a hashtable
$parameters = New-Object -TypeName hashtable
$jsonContent = Get-Content $ParametersFile
    -Raw | ConvertFrom-Json
$jsonContent.parameterValues | Get-Member
    -Type NoteProperty | ForEach-Object {
        $parameters.Add($_.Name,
        $jsonContent.parameterValues.($_.Name))
    }

# deploy
New-AzureResourceGroup
    -Name $ResourceGroupName
    -DeploymentName $DeploymentName
    -Location $Location
    -TemplateFile $TemplateFile
    -TemplateParameterObject $parameters
    -Force
```

The final step is to update the website deployment with the App Settings to access DocumentDb and Redis Cache. The script generates a JSON file with the settings and then calls the `Set-WebsiteConfiguration` function.

```
# generate the appsettigs config file
$JSON = @"
{
  "environmentSettings": {
    "webSite": {
      "name": "$SiteName",
      "location": "$AzureLocation",
      "appSettings": [
        {
          "docdburi": "$DocDbURI",
          "docdbkey": "$DocDbKEY",
          "redisuri": "$RedisURI"
        }
      ]
    }
  }
}
"@

$AppSettingsFile = $Repo
    + "\Automation\Deploy\Scripts\Templates\" + $SiteName
    + "-appsettings.json" $JSON | Set-Content
    -Path $AppSettingsFile

#Update the application settings with values from the JSON file
Set-WebsiteConfiguration $AppSettingsFile
```

■ **Note**   Sample code from Tom Hollander was used to provide this feature of the script. See Tom's post at `http://bit.ly/1NisNsy`.

EXERCISE 6

In this exercise, you will deploy the ConfigM, DeviceM, ProfileM, and RefM microservices.

1. Navigate to the `microservices\config\automation` folder and execute the `03-deploy-configm` script, passing in the `-DeployData:$true` parameter on the command line.

   ```
   > .\03-deploy-configm -DeployData:$true
   ```

2. Navigate to the `microservices\device\automation` folder and execute the `03-deploy-devicem` script, passing in the `-DeployData:$true` parameter on the command line.

   ```
   > .\03-deploy-devicem –DeployData:$true
   ```

3. Navigate to the `microservices\profile\automation` folder and execute the `03-deploy-profilem` script passing in the `-DeployData:$true` parameter on the command line.

   ```
   > .\03-deploy-profilem –DeployData:$true
   ```

4. Navigate to the `microservices\ref\automation` folder and execute the `03-deploy-refm` script passing in the `-DeployData:$true` parameter on the command line.

   ```
   > .\03-deploy-refm –DeployData:$true
   ```

Deploy Biometrics Microservice

The process for deploying the Biometrics microservices is a bit more sophisticated. After packaging, you need to update the Alarm Notification Cloud Service-generated configuration file (.CSCFG) with the connection string information for the Storage Account, Service Bus, and Notification Hub as well as inject the URL for the ConfigM microservice as a configuration setting.

The first step is to dynamically get the connection string information for your storage account.

```
$storagename = $Prefix + "storage" + $Suffix
$storagekey = (Get-AzureStorageKey
    -StorageAccountName $storagename).Primary

$storageconnstr = "DefaultEndpointsProtocol=https;AccountName=$storagename;
AccountKey=$storagekey"
```

Next, you collect the connection string information for Service Bus and Notification Hub.

```
$SBNamespace = $Prefix + "sb" + $Suffix
$NHNamespace = $Prefix + "nh" + $Suffix
$servicebus = Get-AzureSBNamespace
    -Name $SBNamespace -ErrorAction Stop -Verbose
$notificationhub = Get-AzureSBNamespace
    -Name $NHNamespace -ErrorAction Stop -Verbose
$servicebusconnstr = $servicebus.ConnectionString
$notificationhubconnstr = $notificationhub.ConnectionString
```

The Alarm Notification Cloud Service uses both the DeviceM and ProfileM microservices as well as the Biometrics Telemetry API. The service uses the ConfigM microservice to look up the locations of these endpoints at runtime. The one piece of information that the service needs then is the URL to the ConfigM Public API that was provisioned and deployed ealier in the process. This bit of code prepares the URL format so that it can be added as a setting in the configuration file.

```
$ConfigPublicAPI = $Prefix + "ConfigPublicAPI" + $Suffix
$configurl = "https://" + $ConfigPublicAPI +
    ".azurewebsites.net/config"
```

A console application called UpdateCSCFG is provided to update the settings in the Cloud Service configuration files.

```
# path to the config file
$AlarmConfig = $Repo + "\Automation\Deploy\Packages\BiometricAlarmsWorker\
ServiceConfiguration.Cloud.cscfg"

# update the storage connection string setting
Update-CSCFG $repo $AlarmConfig
    "Azure.Storage.ConnectionString"
    $storageconnstr
```

The remaining configuration file updates are omitted for brevity. Once the configuration file is updated, the Cloud Service can be deployed. The script checks to see if there is an existing deployment. If one is not found, the New-AzureDeployment cmdlet is invoked; otherwise the Set-AzureDeployment cmdlet is called. Note the use of the –Slot parameter. You can specify 'Production' or 'Staging' and then manually or through a script flip the deployments when appropriate (i.e. staging to production and production to staging). By default, the scripts deploy to production but you can modify these scripts to provide staging and production support if you need it.

```
$BiometricsAlarmPackage = $Repo + "\Automation\Deploy\Packages\
BiometricAlarmsWorker\AlarmsWorker.cspkg"

# deploy alarm worker cloud service
$deployment = Get-AzureDeployment
    -ServiceName $AlarmServiceName
    -Slot Production
    -ErrorAction silentlycontinue

if ($deployment.Name -eq $null)
{
    New-AzureDeployment -ServiceName $AlarmServiceName
                        -Slot Production
                        -Package $BiometricsAlarmPackage
                        -Configuration $BiometricsAlarmConfig
                        -Label $AlarmServiceName
}
```

97

```
else
{
    Set-AzureDeployment -Upgrade $AlarmServiceName
                        -Slot Production
                        -Package $BiometricsAlarmPackage
                        -Configuration $BiometricsAlarmConfig
                        -Label $AlarmServiceName
}
```

EXERCISE 7

In this exercise, you will deploy the Biometrics microservice.

1. Navigate to the `microservices\biometrics\automation` folder and type the following command:

    ```
    > .\03-deploy-biometrics
    ```

Verifying Data Deployment

You can validate the success of the data upload by using the Azure Preview Portal to view the contents of the DocumentDb databases.

EXERCISE 8

In this exercise, you will validate the deployment of the DocumentDb database collections.

1. Navigate to your DocumentDb instance and select the ConfigM database, and then the Manifest Collection.

2. Click the Document Explorer (see Figure 5-21).

Figure 5-21. *DocumentDb Document Explorer*

3. Click one of the documents in the list. You will see a JSON display for the selected document (see Figure 5-22).

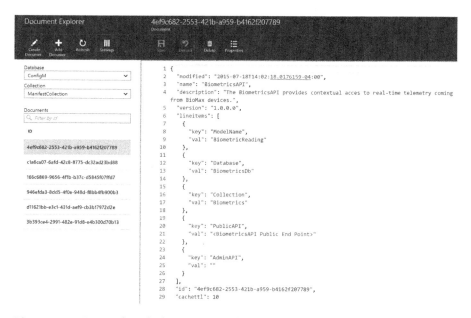

Figure 5-22. *Testing data deployment using the Azure portal*

4. Repeat these steps with the other databases (DeviceM, ProfileM, and RefM).

Verifying Microservice Deployment

The next step in the validation process is to test the functionality of the microservice APIs.

EXERCISE 9

In this exercise, you will validate that each of the microservices is functioning and returning data from DocumentDb.

1. To validate the deployment of the microservices, navigate to an API site such as the RefM Public API. The first page you will see will be the default home page for the service. It provides a simple overview (see Figure 5-23).

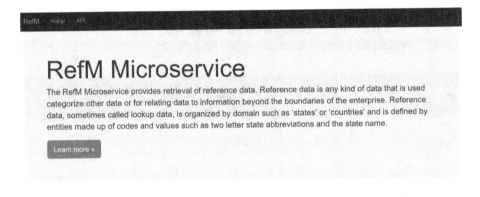

Figure 5-23. *Default page for deployed site*

2. Click the API menu option. You will be shown the generated API documentation that is provided by ASP.NET Web API solutions (see Figure 5-24).

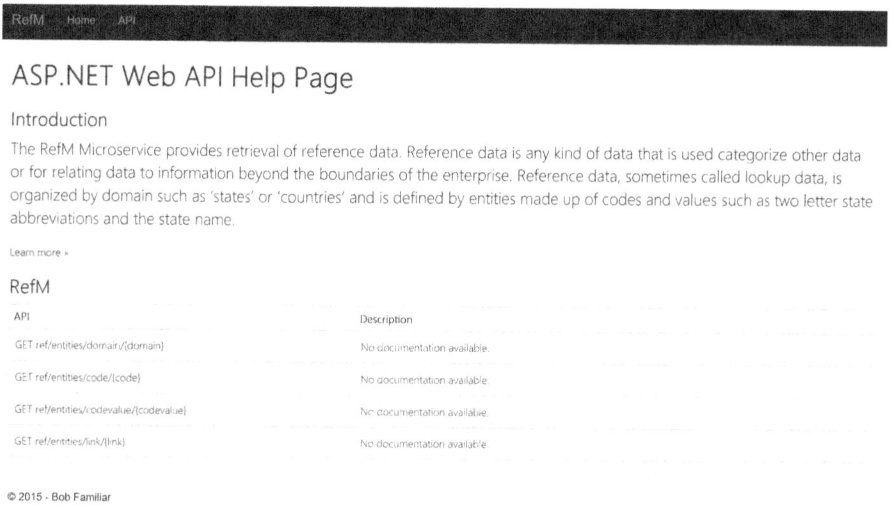

RefM   Home   API

ASP.NET Web API Help Page

Introduction

The RefM Microservice provides retrieval of reference data. Reference data is any kind of data that is used categorize other data or for relating data to information beyond the boundaries of the enterprise. Reference data, sometimes called lookup data, is organized by domain such as 'states' or 'countries' and is defined by entities made up of codes and values such as two letter state abbreviations and the state name.

Learn more »

RefM

API	Description
GET ref/entities/domain/{domain}	No documentation available.
GET ref/entities/code/{code}	No documentation available.
GET ref/entities/codevalue/{codevalue}	No documentation available.
GET ref/entities/link/{link}	No documentation available.

© 2015 - Bob Familiar

Figure 5-24. *ASP.NET Web API Autodocumentation*

3. You can test a call to the RefM microservice using your browser by typing in the route with appropriate parameters. Another approach is to use a tool like Postman. Postman is a very useful tool in the development and debugging of APIs. You provide the URL of the ReST API you want to call, enter any required header values if necessary, and click Send. The tool will display the response from the API, JSON if successful or the error that was encountered. Figure 5-25 depicts a call to the RefM Public API, which returns the list of 50 states in the United States.

```
http://[prefix]refpublicapi[suffix]/ref/entities/
domain/States
```

Figure 5-25. *RefM Public API test results using Postman*

■ **Note** Note You can install Postman by visiting www.getpostman.com/.

---

4. Here is a list of additional endpoints that you can use to validate the microservice deployments:

    • `http://[prefix]configadminapi[suffix].azurewebsites.net/config/manifests` - return a list of all manifests

    • `http://[prefix]configpublicapi[suffix].azurewebsites.net/config/manifests/name/DeviceM` - return the DeviceM manifest

    • `http://[prefix]deviceadminapi[suffix].azurewebsites.net/device/registrations` - return all the device registrations

    • `http://[prefix]devicepublicapi[suffix].azurewebsites.net/device/registrations/model/BIOMAX-HOME` - return all device registrations for BioMax Home units

- `http://[prefix]profileadminapi[suffix].azurewebsites.net/profile/users` - return a list of all user profiles

- `http://[prefix]profilepublicapi[suffix].azurewebsites.net/profile/users/state/MA` - return a list of user profiles in Massachusetts

Note *Prefix* and *suffix* are the parameters that you provided to the provisioning and deployment scripts.

Verifying the Biometrics Microservice

In order to verify the Biometrics microservice, which consists of Event Hub, Stream Analytics, SQL Database, Alarm Notification, and Data Visualization services, there are a few preliminary steps to finalizing the configuration of the reference implementation.

- Use ConfigM Console to update the locations of the microservice APIs to provide runtime discovery.

- Start the Stream Analytics Jobs.

- Use the BioMax Simulator to simulate BioMax devices firing events to Event Hub.

- Connect to SQL Database using SQL Management Studio or an equivalent database query tool to validate that data is flowing into the Biometrics database.

EXERCISE 10

The ConfigM microservice provides a management console for creating and modifying the manifests that document the services running in the environment.

1. Navigate to the `microservices\config\consoles` and open the ConfigMConsole solution in Visual Studio. Start the application.

The ConfigM Management console is a WPF application that lists the manifests that are currently defined in the ConfigM database (See Figure 5-26).

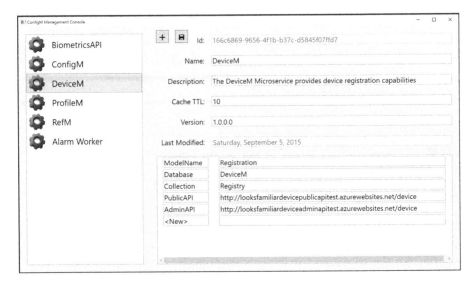

Figure 5-26. ConfigM Management Console

The microservices ConfigM, DeviceM, ProfileM, and RefM have two attributes that you will want to update: PublicAPI and AdminAPI.

2. Update the PublicAPI and AdminAPI properties in the ConfigM, DeviceM, ProfileM, and RefM manifests using the newly minted URLs that were created by the provisioning process.

■ **Note** You can locate those URLs using the Azure portal. Browse the Web Apps and select a Web App to view its details blade (see Figure 5-27). The API is listed under the Essentials sections.

Figure 5-27. *Web App Blade*

3. Update the PublicAPI property in the Biometrics manifest using the ConfigM console.

4. Navigate to the Azure Classic portal and start the biometrics-store Stream Analytics job (see Figure 5-28).

stream analytics

Figure 5-28. *Starting the Stream Analytics job*

In order to test the end-to-end IoT capabilities of the Home Biomedical application, you will need to generate sample device events.

5. Navigate to 6\biometrics\simulator and open the BioMaxSimultor solution in Visual Studio.

6. Start the console application and press Enter to start the process of generating device events (see Figure 5-29).

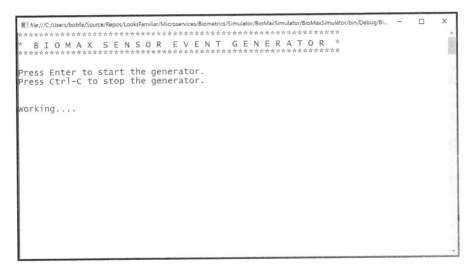

Figure 5-29. BioMax Event Simulator Console

7. Use SQL Management Studio or an equivalent tool to connect to SQL Database and execute a `'select * from biometrics'` query in the BiometricsDb database.

■ **Note**   You can get the connection string information for SQL Database from the Azure portal (see Figure 5-30)

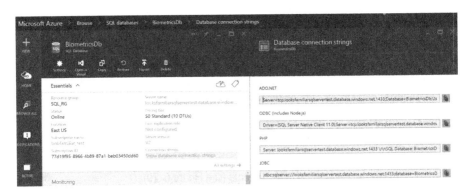

Figure 5-30. SQL Database Connection Strings

■ **Note**   The username and password for the BiometricsDb database are

Username: BioMaxUser001

Password: BioMaxPass001

Using SQL Management Studio, you can connect to the SQL Database instance and set up a 'select * from biometrics' query on the Biometrics table (see Figure 5-31).

Figure 5-31. *Events flowing into SQL Database*

You should see data flowing into the biometrics table. Each run of the query should show that there are more rows coming into the table.

8.   The deployment is now validated. You can stop the BioMax Simulator console app.

■ **Note**   Additional details on Event Hubs, Stream Analytics, Data Visualization, and Alarm Notifications will be covered in Chapter 7.

Summary

In this chapter, you looked at the process of automating the provisioning of Azure resources, building software assets and deploying those software assets to Azure. You examined how this automation could be accomplished using a combination of PowerShell and C#. You completed the process by validating the deployment. The steps you used to learn about the process of automation could themselves be automated. That is left as an exercise for the reader.

Automation is a core tenant of Continuous Delivery. Through automation, you eliminate manual processes, reduce errors and risk, and increase confidence in the quality of your releases. You are also able to provide a consistent, repeatable process that can execute at velocity. SaaS solutions that are built on Azure and leverage a microservice architecture can take advantage of Azure's automation capabilities to provide Continuous Delivery.

■ ■ ■

## CHAPTER 6

Microservice Reference Implementation

Now that the Home Biomedical Reference Implementation has been provisioned, built, and deployed, you can go another level deeper and examine how the individual custom microservices are implemented. To provide some context for the solution, let's review the back story for this product.

The Product

Home Biomedical, a wholly owned subsidiary of LooksFamiliar, Inc., is a leader in commercial grade chemical and blood biometric measurement devices. Home Biomedical is creating a new product for the home health care market that combines blood glucose, heart rate, temperature, and blood oxygen sensors in a handsome, consumer friendly package. The new product will be part of their BioMax product line and will be called the BioMax-Home Edition.

The Epic

The BioMax-Home device will be used by individuals who are under the care of a physician and are participating in a new drug trial. The devices will be provisioned and assigned to each individual. There will be 300 BioMax devices used for the initial trial run. The participants will be based in Boston, New York, and Chicago. The provisioning process will assign the device to each participant by their participant id and log their geo-location.

The device will cloud connect and allow doctors and caregivers to monitor patients/participants in real time while at home. The devices will use biometric sensors to take blood glucose, blood oxygen, temperature, and heart rate readings multiple times per second and send the data to the BioMax-Home cloud application using the participant's home wireless network. The biometric data will be staged for real-time data visualization, stored for archival purposes, and analyzed for alarms that will be logged and will trigger real-time alerts to physician's mobile devices. The real-time data visualization will provide the ability to map the device locations and provide both individual as well as aggregate readings.

The Business Capabilities

From this epic the product team was able to identify these business capabilities for a minimal-viable product (MVP) to be built and tested with a group of patients participating in a pharmaceutical trial (see Figure 6-1):

- **Device Management**: The ability to define a device, its serial number, SKU, and firmware revision, and capture the id of the patient or participant to whom it is assigned.

- **Profile Management**: The ability to capture the profile of a patient/participant including name, address, email, phone, and social network affiliations.

- **Telemetry Ingestion, Transformation, and Routing**: The ability to ingest device messages containing sensor geo-location readings, perform data transformation if needed, and route to various storage mediums for downstream processing.

- **Real-Time Data Visualization**: The ability to project in visual form the data that is streaming in real time from the devices.

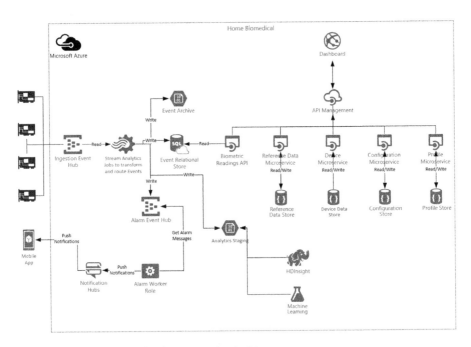

Figure 6-1. *Home Biomedical Microservice Architecture*

The Technical Capabilities

In order to support the features identified for each of the business capabilities, the product team used domain-drive design to identify the bounded contexts of the domain to identify the technical capabilities needed to support the MVP.

- Device Management Service
- User Profile Management Service
- Telemetry Ingestion and Storage Services
- Data Visualization Service

In addition to these business domain services, a set of cross-cutting concerns were identified:

- Discoverability and Configuration
- Reference Data
- Authentication and Authorization

The Azure Resources

Finally, the team mapped these services to Azure Platform Resources. In some cases the entire technical capability is provided by Azure, and in other cases a portion of what is required is provided by the platform. The remaining capabilities will be custom built.

- **Event Hub**: Telemetry Ingestion
- **Stream Analytics**: Telemetry Transformation and Routing
- **Notification Hub**: Real-Time Alerts
- **Blob Storage**: Telemetry Archival
- **SQL Database**: Telemetry Staging
- **DocumentDb**: Storage for Microservice Models
- **Redis Cache**: In-Memory Cache
- **Web Sites**: Containers for Custom ReST APIs and Data Visualization Portal
- **Cloud Services**: Containers for Custom Worker Roles for Instrumentation and Notification

The Custom Microservices

A set of microservice capabilities were also identified:

- Device Management
- Profile Management
- Discoverability and Configuration
- Reference Data

■ **Note** The Internet of Things (IoT) components of the solution will be covered in detail in Chapter 7, specifically Event Hub, Notification Hub, and Stream Analytics.

Microservice Reference Implementation

Each microservice uses the same logical architecture introduced in Chapter 3. You will review the application of this architecture pattern through a code review of the ConfigM microservice (see Figure 6-2).

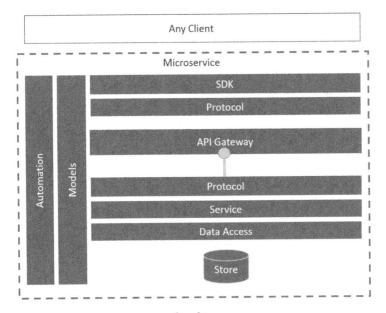

Figure 6-2. *Microservice Logical Architecture*

A review of the implementation of the ConfigM microservice provides a pattern by which all the microservices in the reference implementation are based. Once you understand how ConfigM is implemented, you will understand them all.

One Microservice, Two APIs

One of the first steps in designing a microservice is the definition of the endpoints or API. When defining APIs for microservices, you will discover endpoints that you want to expose for public consumption. You'll also find endpoints that you need but do not want to expose publicly; these are usually administrative operations. You may choose to keep them private or provide them to only a certain class of application.

Reference data is a good example. Reference data, such as the list of states, country codes, or language codes, is read-only data. You do not want to allow just any application to modify this data and corrupt the lookup lists. A public API for reference data could provide read-only access for these lookup lists. A private API would provide maintenance operations such as create, update, and delete. So the end result of defining an API for reference data produces two distinct APIs: one for public consumption that is read-only and one for administrative consumption that provides the complete set of CRUD operations. The APIs together define the entire programmable surface area of the microservice and share the same data model and repository. They are deployed independently, though, to allow for different scale profiles and security concerns.

You may also determine that you want to provide client SDKs for the public and admin APIs as well as monitoring dashboards and management consoles. A microservice, in other words, is more than just a ReST API; it is a software product and as such may provide several APIs, consoles, utilities, etc., to deliver the complete set of capabilities that make up its domain.

■ **Note** The terms *public API* and *admin API* are used throughout the Reference Implementation to distinguish these two API types. The source code for both APIs is placed side by side within the folder structure of Git Repo, and consistent naming standards are used within the build and automation scripts to provide continuity.

Common

As with any development effort, there will always be some common code shared by every component. Your Reference Implementation is no different and provides two common libraries:

- **Wire**: ReST calls, and XML and JSON serialization helper classes that leverage Newtonsoft.JSON

- **Store**: DocumentDb, Redis Cache, and Service Bus helper classes

Wire

The Wire Assembly is a utility class library that provides classes for making ReST calls and for managing serialization to and from JSON and XML.

ModelManager

The ModelManager class is a static class that provides Generics-typed serialization and deserialization methods for both JSON and XML. It uses Newtonsoft's JSON.Net for JSON serialization and the .Net Framework for XML serialization. The methods of the ModelManager class are as follows:

```
// convert JSON to type T
public static T JsonToModel<T>(string objString)

//convert type T to JSON
public static string ModelToJson<T>(T obj)

// convert XMLto type T
public static T XmlToModel<T>(string objString)

// convert type T to XML
public static string ModelToXml<T>(T obj)
```

Rest

The Rest class is a static class that provides Get, Put, Post, and Delete methods given a URL and, where appropriate, a payload.

A typical use of both the ModelManager and Rest classes is to prepare and make a ReST call, and then deal with the JSON payload that is returned.

```
// setup call to retrieve a customer by id
var uri = new Uri("https://api.myapi.com/customers/id/12345");

// make the GET call
var json = Rest.Get(uri);

// convert JSON payload to customer type
var customer = ModelManager.JsonToModel<Customer>(json);
```

■ **Note**   To review both the ModelManager and Rest class implementations, refer to the Wire solution at

```
microservices\common\wire\wire.sln.
```

Store

The Store assembly provides a set of interfaces and classes for persistence of JSON models using DocumentDb, Redis Cache, and Service Bus queue. There is an interface and implementation class for each type of store as well as a Persist interface and implementation that combines DocumentDb and Redis Cache to provide optimized persistence.

Optimized Persistence

Optimizing persistence is not always warranted, but when it is, adding caching can provide the necessary boost in performance. A simple example of this is found in the Persist implementation where the following operations are optimized by leveraging the cache in conjunction with the Dbase class:

- Insert operations are optimized by storing results in the database as well as in cache.

- Select operations are optimized by selecting first from cache and, if not found, then selecting from the database, and then inserting into cache.

- Update operations are optimized by deleting from cache, updating the database, and then inserting into cache.

- Delete operations delete from both cache and the database.

Interfaces

The following are the interfaces:

- **IQueue**: The interface for sending and receiving messages via a store and forward queue

```
public interface IQueue
{
    // connect to a queue
    void Connect(string queueName);

    // read from the queue
    string Read();

    // write to the queue
    void Write(string message);
}
```

115

- **ICache**: The interface that defines in-memory cache operations

```
public interface ICache
{
    // conncet to the cache
    void Connect();

    // insert into the cache
    void Insert(string key, string value, int ttl);

    // check to see if item is in the cache
    bool Exists(string key);

    // update the item in the cache
    void Update(string key, string value, int ttl);

    // get the item from the cache
    string Select(string key);

    // delete the item from the cache
    void Delete(string key);

    // clear the cache
    void Clear();
}
```

- **IDbase**: The interface that defines NoSQL store operations

```
public interface IDbase
{
    // connect to the database
    void Connect(string databaseId, string collectionId);

    // select all type T from the database
    List<T> SelectAll<T>();

    // select T using query
    List<T> SelectByQuery<T>(string query);

    // select T using model id
    List<T> SelectByModelId<T>(string modelid);

    // select T using database id
    T SelectById<T>(string id);

    // select T by name
    T SelectByName<T>(string name);
```

```
    // insert T
    void Insert<T>(T model);

    // update T
    void Update<T>(T model);

    // delete item with key from database
    void Delete(string key);
}
```

- **IPersist**: The interface for optimized persistent store operations

```
public interface IPersist : IDbase
{
    // for caching lists
    void InsertCache<T>(T model);
}
```

Implementation

The following section provides examples of using the Queue, Cache, Dbase, and Persist classes.

Queue

The Queue class encapsulates read and write calls to the Service Bus queue. In order to use the Queue class, your Service Bus connection string must be present in the app.config or web.config file of the client applications.

```
<appSettings>
    <add key="Microsoft.ServiceBus.ConnectionString" value="Endpoint=
    sb://[your-namespace].servicebus.windows.net;SharedAccessKeyName=
    [shared-policy-name];SharedAccessKey=[your-secret]" />
</appSettings>
```

The Queue class can be used to provide loosely coupled messaging between solution components. Here is an example of how to use the Queue class:

```
using LooksFamiliar.Microservices.Common.Wire;
using LooksFamiliar.Microservices.Common.Store;

// create a queue
IQueue queue; = new Queue();

// connect to a queue named 'log'
queue.Connect("log");

// create a message to send - note definition of message class is implied
message = new Message
```

```
{
    subject = "Log Message",
    body = "Customer Registration Complete"
};

// convert message to JSON
var json = ModelManager.ModelToJson<Message>(message);

// write the message to the queue
queue.Write(json);
```

Cache

The Cache class implements insert, update, and delete operations for serialized object models in Redis Cache. Here is an example of how you can use the Cache class to store an object in the Redis Cache. Note that the Customer class has both a unique id and a Cache-Time-To-Live (cachettl) property. The Cache-Time-To-Live tells Redis how long the object will remain available in memory.

```
using LooksFamiliar.Microservices.Common.Wire;
using LooksFamiliar.Microservices.Common.Store;

public class Customer
{
    public Customer()
    {
        id = Guid.NewGuid().ToString();
        cachettl = 5;
    }

    public string id { get; set; }
    public int cachettl { get; set; }
    public string firstname { get; set; }
    public string lastname { get; set; }
}

void InsertCustomerIntoCache(string redisuri, Customer customer)
{
    // create the cache and connect
    ICache cache = new Cache(redisuri);
    cache.Connect();

    // convert the object to json
    var json = ModelManager.ModelToJson<Customer>(customer);

    // customer object will be cached in memory for 5 minutes
    cache.Insert(customer.id, json, customer.cachettl);
}
```

The reverse of this operation is to look up the Customer in the cache by its unique id. If found, Redis returns the JSON for that object. If not found, Redis returns null. Here is an example of how to retrieve a Customer object from the cache:

```
Customer SelectCustomerFromCache(string redisuri, string id)
{
    // create and connect to the cache
    ICache cache = new Cache(redisuri);
    cache.Connect();

    // lookup object in cache
    var json = cache.Select(id);

    // if found return object, otherwise return null
    return json == null ? null : ModelManager.JsonToModel<Customer>(json);
}
```

Dbase

The Dbase class implements the IDbase interface, providing insert, update, delete, and select operations for JSON serialized object models using DocumentDb. In order to uniquely identify your documents in the database, it is recommended that you add a unique identifier to your object model. Combined with the Cache-Time-To-Live, you have the necessary metadata to manage the storage and retrieval of unique objects from both DocumentDb and Redis Cache.

Here is an example of how to store a Customer object in DocumentDb using the Dbase class:

```
void InsertCustomer(string docdburi, string docdbkey, Customer customer)
{
    IDbase dbase = new Dbase(docdburi, docdbkey);
    dbase.Connect("MyDatabase", "MyCollection");
    dbase.Insert<Customer>(customer);
}
```

And here is an example of looking up a Customer by id:

```
Customer SelectCustomer(string docdburi, string docdbkey,  string id )
{
    IDbase dbase = new Dbase(docdburi, docdbkey);
    dbase.Connect("MyDatabase", "MyCollection");
    return dbase.SelectById<Customer>(id);
}
```

Persist

The Persist class exposes the same interface as Dbase but combines the functionality of Dbase and Cache to provide optimized storage operations.

To provide a simple example of how the optimization logic works, here is the previous Customer example expressed using both Dbase and Cache:

```
void InsertCustomer(string docdburi, string docdbkey, string redisuri,
Customer customer)
{
    // create and connect to the database and the cache
    IDbase dbase = new Dbase(docdburi, docdbkey);
    ICache cache = new Cache(redisuri);

    dbase.Connect("MyDatabase", "MyCollection");
    cache.Connect();

    // store the customer in the database
    dbase.Insert<Customer>(customer);

    // store the customer in the cache
    var json = ModelManager.ModelToJson<Customer>(customer);
    cache.Insert(customer.id, json, customer.cachettl);
}

Customer SelectCustomer(string docdburi, string docdbkey, string redisuri,
string id )
{
    // create and connect to the database and the cache
    IDbase dbase = new Dbase(docdburi, docdbkey);
    ICache cache = new Cache(redisuri);

    dbase.Connect("MyDatabase", "MyCollection");
    cache.Connect();

    // lookup the customer in the cache
    var json = cache.Select(id);

    return json == null ? dbase.SelectById<Customer>(id) :
        ModelManager.JsonToModel<Customer>(json);
}
```

The sample above rewritten to use the Persist class would be as follows:

```
void InsertCustomer(string docdburi, string docdbkey, string redisuri,
Customer customer)
{
    IPersist persist = new Persist(new Dbase(docdburi, docdbkey),
    new Cache(redisuri));
```

```
    persist.Connect("MyDatabase", "MyCollection");
    persist.Insert(customer);
}

Customer SelectCustomer(string docdburi, string docdbkey, string redisuri,
string id)
{
    IPersist persist = new Persist(new Dbase(docdburi, docdbkey),
    new Cache(redisuri));
    persist.Connect("MyDatabase", "MyCollection");
    return persist.SelectById<Customer>(id);
}
```

The Persist class demonstrates the use of dependency injection, using interfaces to decouple the Persist class from the Dbase and Cache implementations. Any instances of classes that implement IDbase and ICache are passed in on the call to the constructor.

```
IPersist persist = new Persist(new Dbase(docdburi, docdbkey), new
Cache(redisuri));
```

This technique of creating a loose coupling between a class and its dependencies allows you to easily introduce new implementations of Dbase and Cache without breaking the code. This can be helpful during development where you may have mocked versions of these classes before you have concrete implementations. It also provides you a path to evolve the capabilities of the system with no impact on the classes using those interfaces.

■ **Note** To review the Store classes and interfaces, refer to the Store solution at microservices\common\store\store.sln.

ConfigM - Configuration and Discoverability

In order to provide loose coupling between applications and microservices, there needs to be a mechanism by which the location of services can be determined dynamically at runtime. ConfigM is a microservice that provides configuration and dynamic discoverability of microservices. Applications or microservices that use ConfigM can dynamically look up information about a microservice and use that information to construct a call. This can be useful as microservices move through their deployment pipeline from dev to test to staging and on to production. This data can be managed by the ConfigM microservice and retrieved dynamically at runtime by any service or application that wants to invoke any other service.

ConfigM Model

The ConfigM data model, called Manifest, defines an extensible structure, allowing each registered microservice to store name, description, version number, and last modified date along with any number of configuration line items (see Figure 6-3).

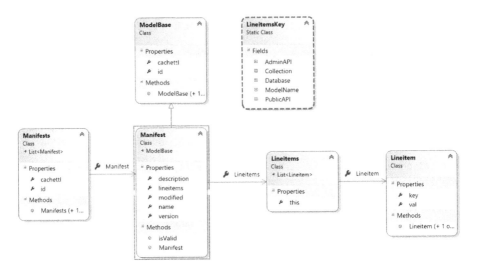

Figure 6-3. *ConfigM Model Manifest*

The line items collection is a list of name-value pairs. Using this collection, you can store all the necessary configuration information that a client of the service may require. If the configuration data needs to be updated, the ConfigM admin API provides an endpoint to update a manifest (see Figure 6-3).

■ **Note**   The ConfigM model solution is located here:

`microservices\config\models\ConfigModels.sln`.

ConfigM Interfaces

ConfigM provides two interfaces, one that defines the public interface and another that defines the admin interface. These interfaces are eventually used to define the APIs that will be exposed over HTTP. Both interfaces reference the same ConfigM models package that defines the ConfigM manifest model. The public interface defines methods for getting a manifest by id and getting a manifest by name.

```
using LooksFamiliar.Microservices.Config.Models;

namespace LooksFamiliar.Microservices.Config.Public.Interface
{
    public interface IConfig
    {
        Manifest GetById(string id);
        Manifest GetByName(string name);
    }
}
```

The admin interface defines methods for creating, updating, deleting, and getting all manifests from the repository.

```
using LooksFamiliar.Microservices.Config.Models;

namespace LooksFamiliar.Microservices.Config.Admin.Interface
{
    public interface IConfigAdmin
    {
        Manifests GetAll();
        Manifest Create(Manifest model);
        Manifest Update(Manifest model);
        void Delete(string id);
    }
}
```

■ **Note**   The ConfigM public and admin interface solutions are located here:

```
microservices\config\public\interface
microservices\config\admin\interface
```

ConfigM Services

The ConfigM services are the implementation of the ConfigM interfaces. This is where the heavy lifting of the microservice is done. If there are any business rules, calculations, or integrations with other services to provide support, it is done here. In the case of ConfigM, the rules are pretty simple; where appropriate, check that the model is valid before committing and return an exception if something goes wrong.

The following code is an example of how the ConfigM service might be used at runtime to look up the location of the ProfileM public API. The rest of the example uses that information to make a ReST call to the ProfileM microservice to get the list of employees in Massachusetts.

```
// instantiate the ConfigM Service
ConfigM configM = new ConfigM(docdburi, docdbkey, redisuri);

// lookup the manifest for the ProfileM Microservice
var manifest = configM.GetByName("ProfileM");

// get the location of the Public API from the manifest and create a uri
new uri = new Uri(manifest.lineitems[LineitemsKey.PublicAPI] + "/users/state/MA" );

// call the API to get all the user profiles of employees in MA
var json = Rest.Get(uri);

// conert the json
UserProfiles userProfiles = ModelManager.JsonToModel<UserProfiles>(json);
```

■ **Note**   The ConfigM public and admin service solutions are located here:

microservices\config\public\service

microservices\config\admin\service

ConfigM APIs

There have been many technology stacks on the Microsoft platform over the years for implementing a service: ASMX, WCF, and Web API, to name but a few. Azure API Apps are the newest option and are currently in preview. They build on the ASP.NET Web API, and introduce new and wonderful ways to define, implement, and deploy APIs. I have standardized on ASP.NET Web API for all the API solutions in the Reference Implementation.

■ **Note**   To learn about Azure API Apps, visit http://bit.ly/1i2utKY. For a primer on ASP.Net Web API, see http://bit.ly/1qLbqSx.

To define the ConfigM public API, a controller class is added to an ASP.NET Web API project. The ConfigPublicService NuGet package is referenced. Referencing this NuGet package automatically pulls in all the NuGet packages that this library has dependencies on. The constructor instantiates the ConfigM Service class and uses the .NET AppSettings class to retrieve the connection string information for DocumentDb and Redis Cache.

When deploying to Azure, web sites have a feature whereby you can store key-value string pairs as part of the configuration information (see Figure 6-4). Azure will retrieve these values for you and make them available through AppSettings at runtime. From a security perspective, this is a nice benefit since sensitive information will never show up as clear text in the web.config file. These settings are automatically applied by the deployment scripts covered in Chapter 5.

Connection strings

The connection strings are hidden	Show connection strings			
docdburi	< Hidden for Security...	Custom	☐	Slot settin
docdbkey	< Hidden for Security...	Custom	☐	Slot settin
redisuri	< Hidden for Security...	Custom	☐	Slot settin
Name	*Value*	SQL D... ∨	☐	Slot settin

Figure 6-4. *Connection Strings Stored in Azure*

```
using System.Web.Http;
using LooksFamiliar.Microservices.Config.Models;
using LooksFamiliar.Microservices.Config.Public.Interface;
using LooksFamiliar.Microservices.Config.Public.Service;

namespace ConfigAPI.Controllers
{
    public class ConfigMController : ApiController
    {
        private readonly IConfig _configM;

        public ConfigMController()
        {
            // the configuration is read from Web.Config when
            // running locally and from the Azure Portal at runt time

            var docdburi = ConfigurationManager.AppSettings["docdburi"];
            var docdbkey = ConfigurationManager.AppSettings["docdbkey"];
            var redisuri = ConfigurationManager.AppSettings["redisuri"];

            this._configM = new ConfigM(docdburi, docdbkey, redisuri);
        }
    }
}
```

The ConfigMController class is updated to define the ReST endpoint routes and then maps them to the matching methods on the ConfigM Service classes. The public API routes are defined in Figure 6-5.

VERB	ROUTE	NOTES
GET	config/manifests/id/{id}	Return a Manifest by its unique Id
GET	config/manifests/name/{name}	Return a Manifest by its name

Figure 6-5. *ConfigM Public API Routes*

The implementation of these routes is

```
[Route("config/manifests/id/{id}")]
[HttpGet]
public Manifest GetById(string id)
{
    return _configM.GetById(id);
}


 [Route("config/manifests/name/{name}")]
 [HttpGet]
 public Manifest GetByName(string name)
 {
     return _configM.GetByName(name);
 }
```

Just like the public API, the ConfigM admin API is implemented by adding a controller class to the solution and by referencing the ConfigAdminService package.

The ConfigMController class is updated to define the ReST endpoint routes and then maps them to the matching methods on the ConfigM Service class.

```
using System.Web.Http;
using LooksFamiliar.Microservices.Config.Admin.Interface;
using LooksFamiliar.Microservices.Config.Admin.Service;
using LooksFamiliar.Microservices.Config.Models;

namespace ConfigAdminAPI.Controllers
{
        public ConfigMController()
        {
            // the configuration is read from Web.Config when
            // running locally and from the Azure Portal at runt time
```

```
        var docdburi = ConfigurationManager.AppSettings["docdburi"];
        var docdbkey = ConfigurationManager.AppSettings["docdbkey"];
        var redisuri = ConfigurationManager.AppSettings["redisuri"];

        this._configM = new ConfigM(docdburi, docdbkey, redisuri);
    }
```

The admin API endpoints are listed in Figure 6-6.

VERB	ROUTE	NOTES
GET	config/manifests	Return all Manifests in the store
GET	Config/manifests/id/{id}	Return all Manifests from cache
POST	config/manifests	Create a Manifest from payload
PUT	config/manifests	Update a Manifest from payload
DELETE	config/manifests/id/{id}	Delete a Manifest by unique Id

Figure 6-6. *ConfigM Admin API Routes*

The implementation of the endpoints is

```
[Route("config/manifests")]
[HttpPost]
public Manifest Create([FromBody] Manifest manifest)
{
    return _configM.Create(manifest);
}

[Route("config/manifests")]
[HttpPut]
public Manifest Update([FromBody] Manifest manifests)
{
    return _configM.Update(manifests);
}

[Route("config/manifests")]
[HttpGet]
public Manifests GetAll()
{
    return _configM.GetAll();
}
```

```
[Route("config/manifests/id/{id}")]
[HttpGet]
public Manifests GetAll(string id)
{
    return _configM.GetAll(id);
}

[Route("config/models/id/{id}")]
[HttpDelete]
public void Delete(string id)
{
    _configM.Delete(id);
}
```

One thing to note is how thin this implementation tier is. This code serves two purposes: it maps the ReST endpoints to the appropriate calls to your service class, and it provides the connection to the cloud-based container for running the microservice.

There is now great flexibility for when another protocol or technology stack enters the picture. If, in the future, you decide to migrate to another technology stack such as API Apps or Service Fabric, or provide a WCF implementation, or choose some other container mechanism, the amount of effort to get there has been minimized.

■ **Note**　The ConfigM public and admin API solutions are located here:

microservices\config\public\api

microservices\config\admin\api

ConfigM SDKs

Once the APIs are deployed it is possible to claim mission accomplished. Any developer who knows how to craft a ReST call and has access to your API can get the job done.

Optionally, you can develop an SDK to create a developer experience that is akin to instantiating a class and calling a method. Understand that once you go down this path, you will be responsible for this code: you will need to keep it in sync with your API, and keep the users of your SDKs informed of new releases. This responsibility is further magnified by the number of programming languages and platforms you choose to support. The upside is you have created an easy-to-use package for adopting your API.

The Reference Implementation SDKs are built for .NET C# clients and are usable from either desktop apps or ASP.NET server-side code.

The ConfigM Public SDK references the same IConfig interface as the ConfigM Public Service, allowing both the ConfigM class in the server solution and the ConfigM class in the SDK solution to remain in sync.

```
using System;
using LooksFamiliar.Microservices.Config.Models;
using LooksFamiliar.Microservices.Common.Wire;
using LooksFamiliar.Microservices.Config.Public.Interface;

namespace LooksFamiliar.Microservices.Config.Public.SDK
{
    public class ConfigM : IConfig
    ...
}
```

The ConfigM SDK class also exposes two public string properties, DevKey and ApiUrl.

```
public string DevKey { get; set; }
public string ApiUrl { get; set; }
```

ApiUrl is a required property and, if not set, the ConfigM class will throw an exception. Use this property to set the base URL of the microservice. The base URL is the part of the address up to but not including the route. For example,

```
http://api.myapi.com/config
```

is the base URL, while

```
/manifests/id/12345
```

is the route.

The following code is an example of using the ConfigM SDK to look up the manifest for a Customer microservice. Once the manifest is in hand, a call to the Customer microservice can be dynamically constructed and invoked.

```
// create the ConfigM SDK class
ConfigM configM = new ConfigM();

// set the Api base Url
configM.ApiUrl = "http://api.myapi.com/config";

// invoke the API to get a manifest by name
Manifest customerManifest = configM.GetByName("CustomerM");

// use manifest to construct a call to the customer API
var approot = customerManifest.lineitems[ LineitemsKey.PublicAPI ];
var  approute = approot + "/id/12345";
var uri = new Uri(approute);
```

```
// invoke the API
var json = Rest.Get(uri);

// instantiate the customer from the JSON payload
var customer = ModelManager.JsonToModel<Customer>(json);
```

The DevKey is an optional property. If you are using Azure API Management to access the API Proxy for a microservice, you will be assigned a developer key. You use this property to provide the developer key to the SDK.

The ConfigM Admin SDK is implemented exactly the same as the Public SDK except that it is based on the ConfigM admin interface.

■ **Note**   ConfigM Public and Admin SDK solutions are located here:

microservices\config\public\sdk

microservices\config\admin\sdk

The ConfigM Administrator Console

Configurability is one of the key elements that we identified in our definition of microservices. In Chapter 2, configurability was defined as follows:

> *…to be reusable and be able to address the needs of each system that chooses to employ its capabilities, a microservice must provide a means by which it can be appropriately molded to the usage scenario.*

You can see examples of this throughout the Azure platform. Every Azure Service has an accompanying dashboard that provides web-based monitoring and configuration user interfaces as well as accompanying ReST APIs for programmability and management.

To demonstrate how to approach creating a dashboard for a microservice, an administrative console for ConfigM is provided. The ConfigM Management Console is a WPF application that uses the ConfigM Admin SDK to implement the administrative operations on ConfigM manifests. In the context of the Reference Implementation, the manifests are used to look up the locations of microservices at runtime.

The app provides a listing of all the manifests in the database and the ability to create new manifests as well as update existing ones. The attributes are configurable, allowing you to add, modify, or delete the information that is used by applications at runtime to dynamically discover and invoke the microservice (see Figure 6-7).

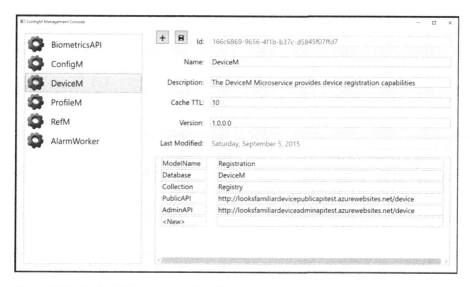

Figure 6-7. ConfigM Management Console

■ **Note** The solution for the ConfigM Management Console is located at `Microservices\Config\ConfigMConsole`.

Summary

In this chapter, the Home Biomedical Reference Implementation was introduced along with the architecture and the approach to defining the microservices that provide cross-cutting and business services. The minimal-viable product (MVP) epic was documented along with a minimal set of requirements and the Azure services needed to implement the MVP. You reviewed the implementation of the ConfigM microservice as a pattern for custom microservices. In the next chapter, you will focus on the IoT aspects of the Reference Implementation that leverage Event Hub, Stream Analytics, SQL Database, Cloud Services, and Web APIs to provide telemetry ingestion, transformation, and data visualization.

CHAPTER 7

■ ■ ■

IoT and Microservices

There are 2 billion PCs in use today across the globe. There are over 10 billion mobile phones. By 2020, it is predicted that there will be over 250 billion devices connected to the Internet. Some of these devices will be new products, but most will be existing things we use every day that will be enhanced with sensors, such as thermostats, cars, eyeglasses, wrist watches, clothing, street lamps, cars, buildings…you name it, it will likely become connected.

Each of these devices will be gathering data through sensors and sending data to the cloud. The amount of data that will be collected will be measured in petabytes, exabytes, and zettabytes. In other words, IoT is not just about devices but also about data, a lot of data. The reason that we want to collect all this data is to extract knowledge, to provide real-time visualization and data feeds, and to perform historical and predictive analytics that will drive business decisions at velocity and provide real-time notification and status.

IoT Capabilities

To fully realize an IoT solution, several capabilities will be required. These capabilities include the following:

> **Device Management**: The device, upon initialization, will want to establish a relationship with the cloud environment, usually through its unique identifier, such as a serial number, so that the business is notified that the device is active. The business will also want the ability to send commands to the device for the purposes of providing software updates or updating local data caches.

> **Telemetry Ingestion**: Devices may be sending multiple messages a second, and there may be hundreds to thousands of devices or more, which would result in 10's of thousands to possibly millions of messages a day. The cloud platform provides high-volume message ingestion using a single logical endpoint.

> **Transformation and Storage**: Once the messages arrive, the cloud provides a mechanism to select, transform, and route messages to various storage mediums for the purpose of archival and staging for downstream processing.

Status and Notifications: The cloud solution will want to provide the ability to visualize the status of the message pool in real time through tabular or graphical UI components. In addition, some messages may contain information of an alert status so the IoT solution must provide a mechanism for real-time notifications.

Analytics and Data Visualization: The value of collecting so much data in a continuous fashion is to build up an historical record for the purpose of performing analytics to glean business insight. Traditional data warehouse techniques or more modern map-reduce and predictive analytics mechanisms can be employed.

Azure IoT Services

Microsoft provides you two approaches to realizing your IoT solutions:

- Custom Development – build from scratch using a combination of IoT Hub, Stream Analytics and Event Hub along with other Azure resources, custom configuration and code to deliver a complete product

- Scripted Scenarios – leverage pre-scripted starter configurations for business scenarios such as remote monitoring and predictive maintenance and combine with custom configuration and code to create a finished product

Custom Development

The custom development approach will leverage Azure IoT Hub, Azure Stream Analytics and Azure Event Hub for device management, telemetry ingestion, transformation and routing. The Home Biomedical Reference Implementation is an example of this custom development approach. Its use of Event Hub for telemetry ingestion from the home biomedical devices and Stream Analytics for message transformation, alarm state identification and routing is detailed later in this chapter. First let's take a look at the newest service available from Microsoft for IoT called IoT Hub.

IoT Hub

In October 2015, Microsoft announced the general availability of IoT Hub. IoT Hub is a fully managed service that enables:

- Reliable device-to-cloud and cloud-to-device hyper-scale messaging

- Secure communications using per-device security credentials and access control

- Device libraries for popular languages and platforms

IoT Hub provides device registration, command and control and symmetric key management for secure authentication on a per-device basis. To provision IoT Hub, from the Azure Portal click New (+), Internet of Things, Azure IoT Hub. The IoT Hub creation blade appears. The default configuration uses the S1 pricing and scale tier and defines 1 unit of scale. Scaling is done by entering a number of units where each unit supports up to 500 devices. You can have up to 200 units for a maximum of 100K devices per IoT Hub and the ability to ingest 50K messages per day. The S2 pricing tier provides up to 1.5 million messages per day (see Figure 7-1).

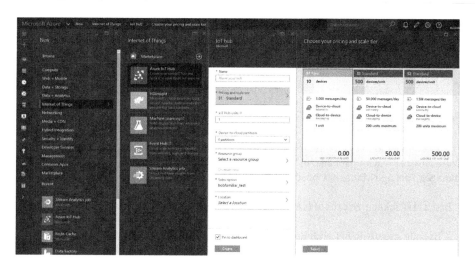

Figure 7-1. *IoT Hub Creation Blade*

Once the IoT Hub is provisioned, you can register devices with the hub so that they can authenticate and send and receive messages. The device provisioning process will be unique to your business and may involve integration with existing systems to align serial numbers, customer information, etc. For demonstration purposes, a sample device registration console application is provided that leverages the ConfigM and DeviceM microservices to register the existing 300 Home Biomedical devices with IoT Hub.

■ **Note**   To use this console app, you will need to provision an IoT Hub and update the sample with the connection string information. The sample solution can be found in IoTHub\ IoTHubDeviceRegistration.

The IoT Hub connections string information can be found by clicking Settings, Shared Access Policies and selecting the policy of interest (see Figure 7-2). The sample application uses the 'iothubowner' policy.

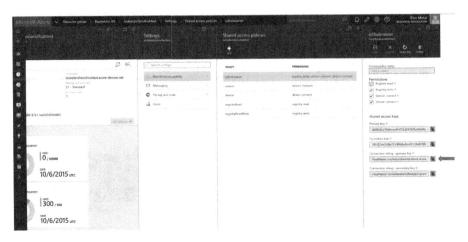

Figure 7-2. IoT Hub Connection String Blade

To connect to IoT Hub and register a device, you need to reference the Micrososft Azure Devices NuGet package. In Visual Studio, select the Tools menu, NuGet Package Manager, Package Manager Console and type in this command:

```
> Install-Package Microsoft.Azure.Devices -Pre
```

In code, create an IoT Hub RegistryManager object passing in the connection string from the App.Config file and call the AddDeviceAsync() method passing in a unique id for the device.

```
// initialize the IoT Hub registration manager
RegistryManager registryManager;
registryManager = RegistryManager.CreateFromConnectionString(
        ConfigurationManager.AppSettings["IoTHubConnStr"]);

// register a device
Device device;
device = await registryManager.AddDeviceAsync(new Device("MyDeviceId"));
```

Once the devices have been registered, you can see the number of devices in the IoT Hub registry on the IoT Hub management blade (see Figure 7-3).

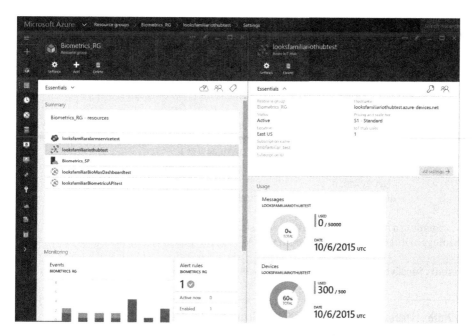

Figure 7-3. *IoT Hub Blade showing 300 registered devices*

Once devices are registered, they can make secure connections to IoT Hub and send and receive messages. IoT device SDKs are available and supported for a variety of languages and platforms including C for Linux distributions, Windows, and RTOS and managed languages such as C#, Java, and JavaScript.

If your solution cannot use the device SDKs, IoT Hub exposes a public protocol that enables devices to use the HTTP 1.1 and AMQP 1.0 protocols. Using the Azure IoT Protocol Gateway component, you can also extend IoT Hub to provide support for MQTT v3.1.1. You can run the Azure IoT Protocol Gateway in the cloud or on premises, and extend it to support custom protocols.

■ **Note**   The Azure IoT Protocol Gateway can be found on GitHub: `https://github.com/` `Azure/azure-iot-protocol-gateway`.

In order to connect to IoT Hub and send messages, you need to reference the Micrososft Azure Devices Client NuGet package. In Visual Studio, select the Tools menu, NuGet Package Manager, Package Manager Console and type in this command:

```
> Install-Package Microsoft.Azure.Devices.Client –Pre
```

The client SDK will use the IoT Hub Uri along with the symmetric key assigned the device to make the secure connection. The Uri can be found on the IoT Hub Blade and has the format [iot-hub-name].azure-devices.net.

```
// get the device from the registry
device = await _registryManager.GetDeviceAsync("MyDeviceId");

// create a connection to the IoT Hub using the Uri and the symmetric key
DeviceClient client= DeviceClient.Create(
    ConfigurationManager.AppSettings["IoTHubUri"],
    new DeviceAuthenticationWithRegistrySymmetricKey(
        "MyDeviceId",
        device.Authentication.SymmetricKey.PrimaryKey));
```

Sending a message to IoT Hub is now straight forward. You collect the sensor readings of interest and call the SendEventAsync() method of the DeviceClient class:

```
Client.SendEventAsync(new Message(Encoding.ASCII.GetBytes(json))).Wait();
```

■ **Note** There is a version of the BioMax Simulator that demonstrates connecting and sending messages to IoT Hub located in IoTHub\BioMaxSimulator-IoTHub.

Scripted Scenario

IoT Suite is a solution-focused offering from Microsoft that provides a point and click approach to provisioning a starter kit for various IoT scenarios. Microsoft provides two scripted scenarios at the time of this writing:

- Remote Monitoring Solution – Provides device management, alerting and notification, telemetry ingestion, data visualization and device geolocation.

- Predictive Maintenance – Using Azure IoT capabilities along with Azure Machine Leaning, provides failure prediction, failure detection, failure type classification, and recommendation of mitigation or maintenance actions after failure.

IoT Suite

To provision an IoT Suite solution, you will need an Azure subscription and then visit https://www.azureiotsuite.com/. From this page you can provision a new solution. As you can see in Figure 7-4, I have already provisioned a Remote Monitoring solution. If I click on the tile, I can get links to the GitHub repository from which the solution was provisioned and guidance on how to customize. I can also de-provision the solution right from this page.

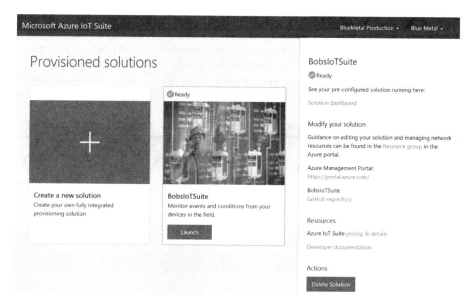

Figure 7-4. *Azure IoT Suite Landing Page*

If I click the 'Launch' button, I am brought to the Dashboard. From here I can see a list of simulated provisioned devices, data streaming from those devices, a map depicting where they are physically located and a menu on the right that provides access to forms for updating the ingestion rules for alerts. In addition there is an add device button (+) in the lower left hand corner to provision additional devices (see Figure 7-5).

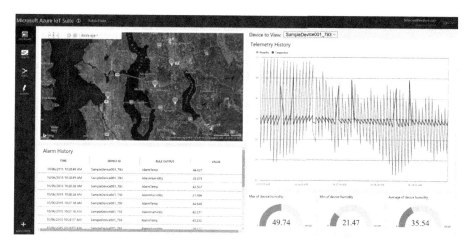

Figure 7-5. *Azure IoT Suite Dashboard*

In the Azure Portal (see Figure 7-6), you will find a new resource group has been created and all of the Azure resources associated with this solution are listed there including an IoT Hub, a DocumentDb database, an Event Hub and three Stream Anlatyics Jobs which you can edit at will. Also, as noted before, you have complete access to the source code and PowerShell scripts for the generated solution on GitHub so that you can configure, customize and extend as needed.

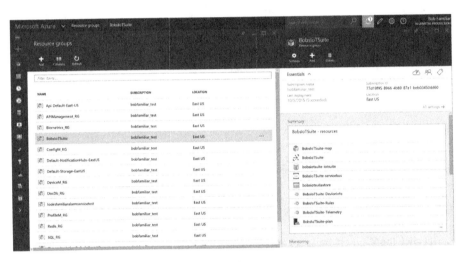

Figure 7-6. *Resource Group listing provisoned services*

The Home Biomedical Reference Implementation, in its current form, demonstrates a custom development approach using Event Hub and Stream Analytics. In the next section of the book, we delve into the details of the reference implementation's IoT capabilities.

The Reference Implementation IoT Capabilities

The Home Biomedical Reference Implementation provides an example of how one can incorporate IoT capabilities into a larger solution. The Reference Implementation uses Microsoft's IoT stack, consisting of Event Hub and Stream Analytics for telemetry ingestion, data transformation, and routing to SQL Database. Real-Time notifications are provided using Event Hub, a custom Event Hub Consumer Cloud Service called Biometrics Alarm Worker, and Notification Hub. Real-time data visualization is provided through a custom API combined with SignalR, which uses Web Sockets to push updates to a web front end (see Figure 7-7).

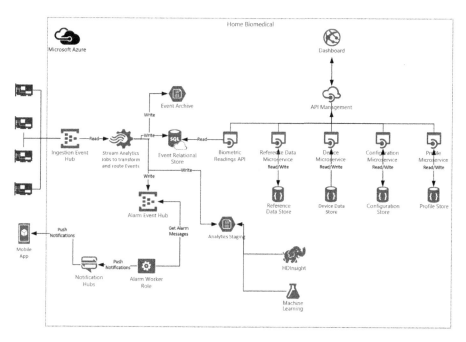

Figure 7-7. Home Biomedical Microservice Architecture

Device Management

The DeviceM provides a device registry for provisioning and associating devices with patients and/or participants in pharmaceutical trials. The administrative API provides create, update, and delete operations as well as a get all, which returns all registrations in the store. The public API defines get by id, which is the serial number of the device, get by participant id, which is the person the device is assigned to, and get by model, which returns all registrations for a device of a particular model (see Figure 7-8).

Public API

VERB	ROUTE	NOTES
GET	device/registrations/id/{id}	Get a device registration by device id (serial number)
GET	device/registrations/participant/{id}	Get a device by participant id (assignment to end user)
GET	device/registrations/model/{model}	Get all registrations by model

Admin API

VERB	ROUTE	NOTES
GET	device/registrations	Get all device registrations
POST	device/registrations	Create (provision a new device)
PUT	device/registrations	Update a device registration
DELETE	device/registrations/id/{id}	Delete a device registration

Figure 7-8. DeviceM API

The DeviceM model is called Registration. A device registration contains the device serial number (id), product line, model, and version and firmware revision. In addition, the id of the patient or participant is stored at the time the device is provisioned (see Figure 7-9).

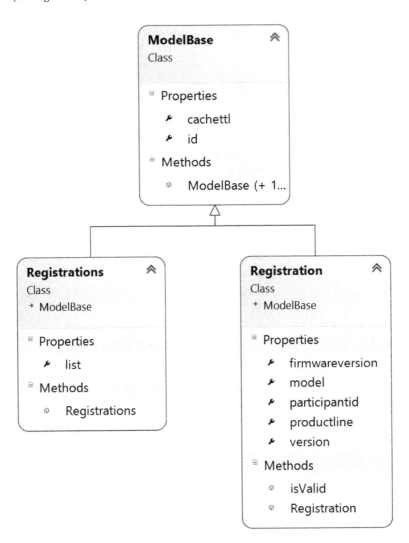

Figure 7-9. DeviceM Model Registration

■ **Note**   The solutions related to the DeviceM microservice can be found in Microservices\Device.

Telemetry Ingestion

Event Hubs is a highly scalable publish-subscribe event ingestor that can intake millions of events per second so that you can process and analyze the massive amounts of data produced by connected devices and applications. Event Hub is configured with some number of partitions, each partition being able to ingest up to 1MB of data per second. By default, Event Hub is configured with 4 partitions. You can only specify the number of partitions at create time. The value can be set to as low as 2 or as high as 32.

Event Hub partitions are able to ingest up to 1MB of data or 1,000 events per second, whichever state is arrived at first. In high-volume telemetry ingestion scenarios, 1,000 messages usually come first because most messages are small. An Event Hub is created with 4 partitions by default. That value can be set to as low as 2 and as high as 32 but only at Event Hub creation. You can't change the number of partitions after the fact. Event Hub is available in basic and standard modes. Both modes provide the same throughput capabilities. Standard mode supports more consumer groups, brokered connections, and additional storage.

A partition is an ordered sequence of events that is held in a repository (see Figure 7-10). As newer events arrive, they are added to the end of this sequence. Events are kept in the repository for a length of time that is configurable. The default is 1 day but it can be set up to 7 days; 1 to 3 days is customary. Once a message's time-to-live has expired, it is removed from the Event Hub repository.

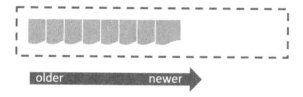

Figure 7-10. *Event Hub Partition Model*

The BioMax-Home Device Simulator

In order to test IoT services, it is necessary to develop an event simulator. Event simulators allow the team responsible for the cloud services to move forward with their development when the devices themselves are not available or do not yet exist. The simulators generate sample telemetry and exercise device provisioning, firmware downloads, and other command and control operations.

Developing device simulators with Event Hub is very straightforward. You use the Service Bus client SDK and add the connection information supplied in the Azure portal to define configuration settings for the endpoint and the name of the Event Hub. You create an object that represents the message you want to send, like sensor readings for a device, fill the object with simulated sensor-reading data, serialize the message to JSON, and send it to the endpoint using the client SDK.

The BioMaxSimulator solution uses the ConfigM Public SDK to look up the locations of the ProfileM Public API and the DeviceM Admin API. The DeviceM Admin SDK is initialized with the endpoint for that service and is used to retrieve the entire device registry. It does this so it can simulate readings coming from the 300 participants in the pharma trial.

```
// instantiate the SDK clients
_config = new ConfigM();
_registry = new DeviceM();
_profiles = new ProfileM();

// get the URL to ConfigM service from the config file
_config.ApiUrl = ConfigurationManager.AppSettings["ConfigM"];

// lookup the manifests for the
// DeviceM and ProfileM microservices
var deviceManifest = _config.GetByName("DeviceM");
var profileManifest = _config.GetByName("ProfileM");

// retrieve their API locations
_registry.ApiUrl = deviceManifest.lineitems[LineitemsKey.AdminAPI];
_profiles.ApiUrl = profileManifest.lineitems[LineitemsKey.PublicAPI];

// get the device registry from the device microservice
_devices = _registry.GetAll();
```

The configuration settings for Service Bus and Event Hub are read from configuration and the Event Hub client is initialized:

```
var bus = ConfigurationManager.AppSettings["servicebus"];
var hubname = ConfigurationManager.AppSettings["eventhub"];
var hub = EventHubClient.CreateFromConnectionString( bus, hubname);
```

The DeviceMessage class is used to construct the JSON messages that will be sent to the Event Hub (see Figure 7-11). The class contains the id of the device, the id of the participant that is using the device, the longitude and latitude of where the device is located, a timestamp of when the sensor readings were taken, and a list of sensor readings. The device will take four readings: Glucose, Heart Rate, Temperature, and Blood Oxygen levels as defined by the SensorType enum. This simulator will generate sample readings for these four biometrics.

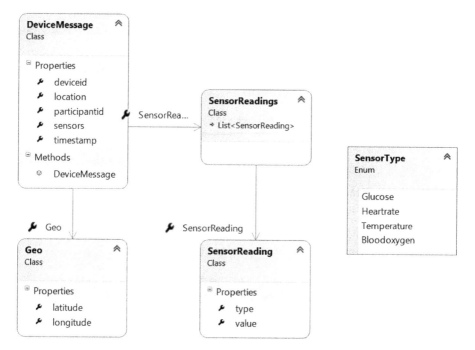

Figure 7-11. *The DeviceMessage Class*

This data model will serialize to JSON as follows:

```
{
  "deviceid": "03015126-aef7-49a3-9a01-1946d98e1383",
  "participantid": "cd57ce66-2065-4bdc-b4d3-ecfb0a5a704f",
  "location": { "longitude": -71.063562, "latitude": 42.290349 },
  "sensors": [
    { "type": 0, "value": 182.0 },
    { "type": 1, "value": 97.0 },
    { "type": 2, "value": 103.0 },
    { "type": 3, "value": 84.0 }
  ],
  "timestamp":"2015-07-13T16:42:16.6125201-04:00"
}
```

The device simulator program enters a loop and generates simulated readings several times a second. The messages are serialized and sent to Event Hub.

```
while (true)
{
    try
    {
        var deviceReading = new DeviceMessage();

        // randomly select a device from the registry
        var device = _devices.list[random.Next(0, 299)];

        // lookup the participant from the profile microservice
        var participant = _profiles.GetById(device.participantid);

        deviceReading.deviceid = device.id;
        deviceReading.participantid = participant.id;

        deviceReading.location.latitude = participant.location.latitude;
        deviceReading.location.longitude = participant.location.longitude;

        // generate simulated sensor reaings
        var glucose = new SensorReading
        {
            type = SensorType.Glucose,
            value = random.Next(70, 210)
        };

        var heartrate = new SensorReading
        {
            type = SensorType.Heartrate,
            value = random.Next(60, 180)
        };

        var temperature = new SensorReading
        {
            type = SensorType.Temperature,
            value = random.Next(98, 105) + (.1 * random.Next(0, 9))
        };

        var bloodoxygen = new SensorReading
        {
            type = SensorType.Bloodoxygen,
            value = random.Next(80, 100)
        };

        deviceReading.sensors.Add(glucose);
        deviceReading.sensors.Add(heartrate);
```

```
        deviceReading.sensors.Add(temperature);
        deviceReading.sensors.Add(bloodoxygen);

        deviceReading.timestamp = DateTime.Now;

        // serialize the message to JSON
        var json = ModelManager.ModelToJson<DeviceMessage>(deviceReading);
        // send the message to EventHub
        eventHubClient.Send(new EventData(Encoding.UTF8.GetBytes(json)));
    }
    catch (Exception exception)
    {
        Console.ForegroundColor = ConsoleColor.Red;
        Console.WriteLine("{0} > Exception: {1}", DateTime.Now,
        exception.Message);
        Console.ResetColor();
    }

    Thread.Sleep(100);
}
```

This code is meant to simulate the code executing on a device. In the real world, many of these devices are running a non-Windows OS such as Linux or Linux variants and the code would most likely be written in C. Microsoft provides a C library for Event Hub using the AMQP protocol and has expanded the number of client libraries with the recent release of IoT Hub. Note that Windows 10 IoT is now available and Microsoft licenses that OS for free on physical devices that are 9 inches or less in diameter.

■ **Note**   To review the simulator source code refer to the following solution: Microservices\Biometrics\Simulator\BioMaxSimulator.

Telemetry Transformation and Storage

Stream Analytics provides low-latency, highly available, elastic event processing over streaming data. Stream Analytics marries extremely well with Event Hub, allowing you to connect to and consume events in the repository based on the properties and values in the JSON message as well as temporal properties such as arrival time. Once messages are selected, they can be directed to one or more storage locations such as Blob Storage, Table Storage, DocumentDb and SQL Database, or sent to another Event Hub for further processing.

To get started with Stream Analytics, you create and configure one or more Stream Analytics jobs (see Figure 7-12). You can do this in either the Classic Portal or the Preview Portal. When creating a job, you specify a unique name, the region the job runs in, and a monitoring storage location.

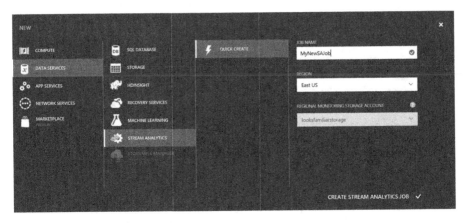

Figure 7-12. *Create Stream Analytics Job*

From the Azure Portal, you can then configure the input, output, and query settings for the Stream Analytics job (see Figure 7-13). Sources of data input can come from Event Hubs or Blob Storage. When defining an input, you provide an alias that will be used in the query ('input' for example). You can also configure the format of the incoming messages, specifying JSON, CSV, or Avro. Avro is a compact and efficient binary file format that leverages JSON for describing Hadoop MapReduce data sets.

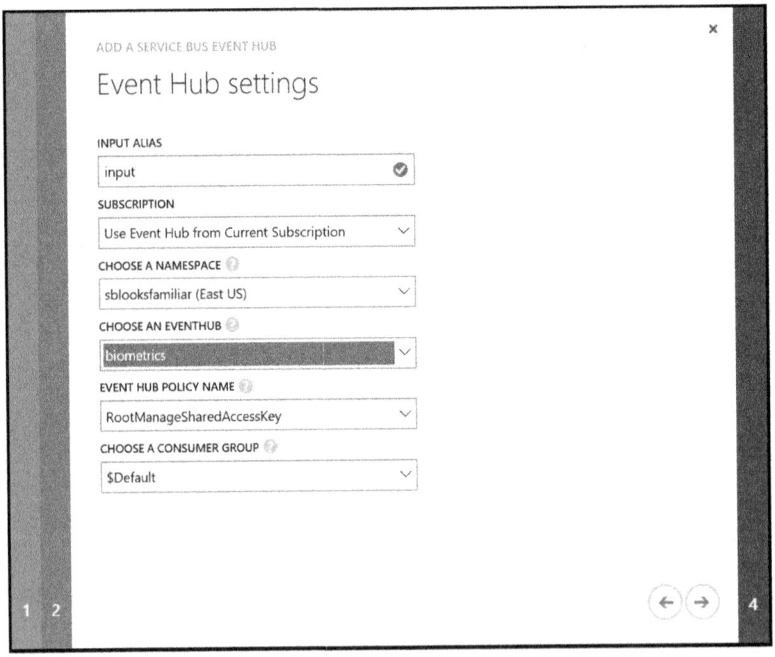

Figure 7-13. *Stream Analytics Job Input Settings for Event Hub*

When you define an output, you provide an alias and then select an output target. The current set of Stream Analytics Outputs includes SQL Database, DocumentDb, Table Storage, Blob Storage, PowerBI, Event Hub, Service Bus queues, and Service Bus topics (see Figure 7-14).

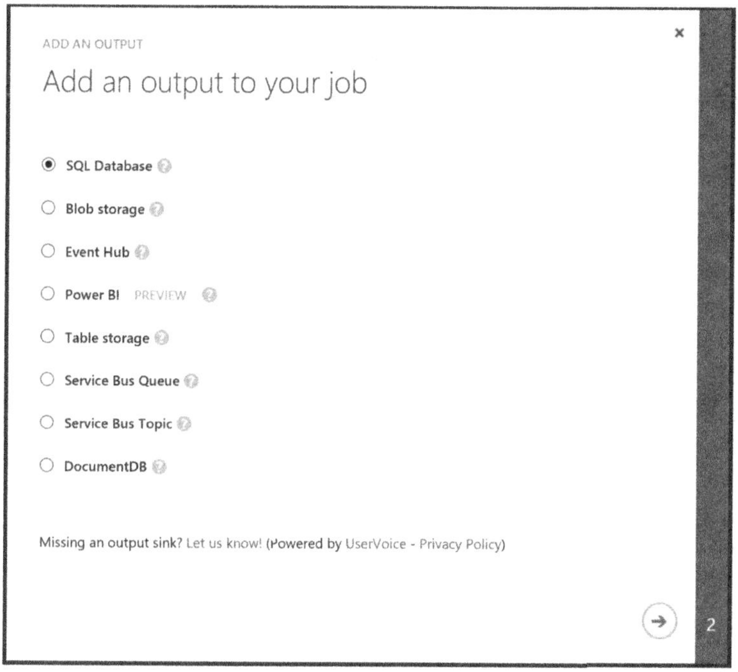

Figure 7-14. *Stream Analytics Job Output Settings*

When configuring SQL Database output, you will be asked to provide the database table name and the login credentials for the database. Note that the table definition in SQL Database must match the columns being selected in the query. In addition, the table must be defined with a clustered index.

Here is the DDL for the SQL Database table that is used by the Reference Implementation:

```
CREATE TABLE[dbo].[biometrics] (
      [deviceid] [char](256) NOT NULL,
      [participantid] [char](256) NOT NULL,
      [longitude] float NOT NULL,
      [latitude] float NOT NULL,
      [reading] datetime NOT NULL,
      [type] bigint NOT NULL,
      [value] float NOT NULL)

CREATE CLUSTERED INDEX[biometrics] ON[dbo].[biometrics] ( [deviceid] ASC )
```

Stream Analytics Queries

Stream Analytics queries are SQL syntax statements that are able to select events based on criteria that includes values in the event, time, and the particular partition where they reside. The Reference Implementation defines six queries:

> **biometrics-blob**: Grab all incoming device messages and send to blob storage using a CSV file format.

> **biometrics-store**: Grab all incoming device messages and send to SQL Database for downstream application integration.

> **glucose-alarms**: Grab only messages that have a glucose reading that is out of bounds and send to the alarms Event Hub endpoint.

> **heartrate-alarms**: Grab only messages that have a heart rate reading that is out of bounds and send to the alarms Event Hub endpoint.

> **temperature-alarms**: Grab only messages that have a temperature reading that is out of bounds and send to the alarms Event Hub endpoint.

> **bloodoxygen-alarms**: Grab only messages that have a blood oxygen reading that is out of bounds and send to the `alarms` Event Hub endpoint.

Each query has a similar structure. Let's looks at one of the alarm queries and dissect its function.

```
1   WITH Device as (SELECT * from input)
2   SELECT
3       Device.deviceid,
4       Device.participantid,
5       Device.location.longitude,
6       Device.location.latitude,
7       Device.timestamp,
8       DeviceSensors.ArrayValue.type,
9       DeviceSensors.ArrayValue.value
10  INTO
11      output
12  FROM
13      Device
14  CROSS APPLY GetElements(Device.sensors) AS DeviceSensors
15  WHERE
16      ((DeviceSensors.ArrayValue.type = 1) AND
         (DeviceSensors.ArrayValue.value > 180))
```

Line 1: Get the next batch of messages from input and create the alias Device to refer to an individual message.

Lines 2 through 9: Select the data of interest. Note the use of the "." (dot) dereference to select into the JSON structure.

Lines 10 and 11: Identify the output by alias.

Lines 12 and 13: Specify where the data is coming from, in this case Device.

Line 14: The CROSS APPLY function allows you to flatten out an array. The end result is that there will be a unique output message for each element in the array.

Lines 15 and 16: The where clause specifies that you are only interested in messages that contain a glucose (type = 1) value that is out of range (value > 180).

Stream Analytics has a feature that allows you to test your queries before putting them into action. This is a very useful feature and should not be overlooked when developing with Stream Analytics. First, let's see how you can test the biometrics-store Stream Analytics query (see Figure 7-15).

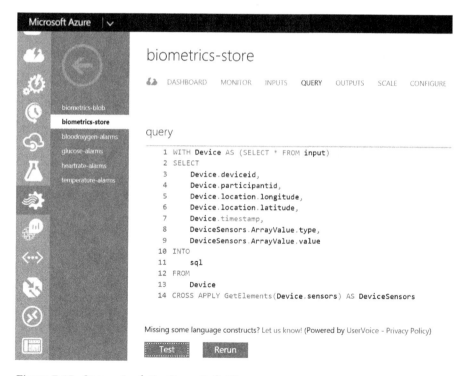

Figure 7-15. Stream Analytics Query Definition

When you click the Test button, a dialog pops up and you can browse to a JSON file that may contain one or more sample JSON messages. When you click Ok, the query is run against the input file and the results are displayed on the page. You can also download the results to a spreadsheet for further analysis. As you can see from the output in Figure 7-16, the query processed a single incoming device message and created four output rows.

Figure 7-16. *Stream Analytics Test Output*

Now let's see what happens when you run a message through the blood oxygen alarm query of a blood oxygen value that is out of range (see Figure 7-17).

Figure 7-17. *Stream Analytics Output for Alarm Query*

Note that when messages contain out-of-bound values, the new alarm message event with the out-of-bound value is sent to the `alarms` Event Hub for processing. By routing alarm messages to a new Event Hub, you can create a real-time notification process.

Real-Time Notifications

A service that reads from an Event Hub is called a consumer. Stream Analytics, for example, is an Event Hub consumer. It is also possible to create custom Event Hub consumers. As you have seen, Stream Analytics can output to Event Hub, giving you the ability to create a cascading set of Event Hub repositories and Event Hub consumers, which may be useful if you need to run custom business logic on a subset of the incoming messages. Dealing with alarm states is one such scenario.

In the case of alarms, you want to do be able to redirect messages to Notification Hub to provide push notification to mobile devices and log the alarms to SQL Database for reporting purposes. Notification Hub is another service available in Azure Service Bus. Its purpose is to provide push notifications to registered applications. A push notification is a dynamic message that arrives on a device in the form of a badge, toast, or tile message. The applications that can receive push notifications can be running on Windows, Apple, Google, Amazon, or Baidu devices.

A Notification Hub defines a namespace within which one or more push notification hubs can be defined. After you create a notification hub, you can add the necessary certificate and client secret settings for each of the platforms that you want to target (see Figure 7-18).

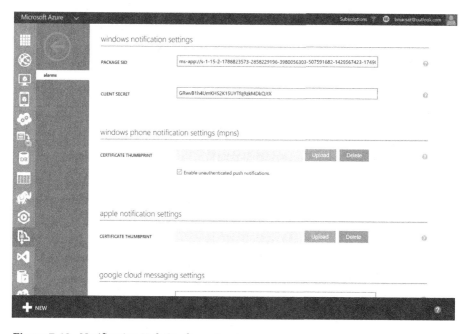

Figure 7-18. *Notification Hub Configuration*

The Biometrics Alarm Notification cloud service connects the dots between the alarm's Event Hub and the alarm's Notification Hub. It will log the alarm to SQL Database using the Biometrics API and send push notifications to a Windows Store application using a push notification hub called alarms. The alarm's Notification Hub is defined within the alarms-ns namespace (see Figure 7-19).

Figure 7-19. *Reference Implementation Notification Hub*

Biometrics Alarm Worker

Upon startup, the Biometrics Alarm Worker instantiates an Event Hub Client, the same client that the BioMax Simulator leverages, to connect to the alarms Event Hub. An EventProcessorHost is created. This class provides an event-driven model for receiving events from an Event Hub endpoint.

```
// the name of the event hub to receive events from
const string eventHubName = "alarms";

// get the service bus connection string from configuration
var serviceBusConnectionString = RoleEnvironment.
GetConfigurationSettingValue(
        "Azure.ServiceBus.ConnectionString");

// get the storage connection string from configuration
var storageConnectionString = RoleEnvironment.GetConfigurationSettingValue(
        "Azure.Storage.ConnectionString");

// define the transport type as AMQP - advanced message queue protocol
var builder = new ServiceBusConnectionStringBuilder(serviceBusConnection
String);
builder.TransportType = TransportType.Amqp;

// create the event hub client
var eventHubReceiveClient = EventHubClient.CreateFromConnectionString(
        builder.ToString(), eventHubName);

// get the default consumer group
var eventHubConsumerGroup = eventHubReceiveClient.GetDefaultConsumerGroup();
```

```
// create the EventProcessorHost
var eventProcessorHost = new EventProcessorHost( "AlarmsWorker",
    eventHubName,
    eventHubConsumerGroup.GroupName,
    builder.ToString(),
    storageConnectionString);
```

```
// register the MessageProcessor class so it recieves the incoming events
eventProcessorHost.RegisterEventProcessorAsync<MessageProcessor>();
```

The EventProcessorHost will route incoming events to a class that implements the IEventProcessor interface. Your solution defines a class called MessageProcessor that implements the IEventProcessor interface. This class encapsulates the work that is necessary to prepare a push notification message and send it to the Notification Hub.

The OpenAsync() method uses two of your microservice SDKs, ConfigM and ProfileM. ConfigM is used to retrieve the manifests for ProfileM and Biometrics microservices. ProfileM is used to look up the details for the study participant who raised the alarm event and the Biometrics API is used to log the alarm messages to SQL Database. This method also creates the connection to the Notification Hub.

```
_config = new ConfigM
{
    ApiUrl = "<path to the config public api service>"
};

Manifest profileManifest = _config.GetByName("ProfileM");

_profile = new ProfileM
{
    ApiUrl = profileManifest.lineitems["PublicAPI"]
};

var biometricsManifest = _config.GetByName("BiometricsAPI");
_biometricsApi = biometricsManifest.lineitems["PublicAPI"] + "/alarm";

// connect to notification hub
var hub = NotificationHubClient.CreateClientFromConnectionString(
        RoleEnvironment.GetConfigurationSettingValue(
            "Azure.NotificationHub.ConnectionString"),
        RoleEnvironment.GetConfigurationSettingValue(
            "NotificationHubName"));
```

The ProcessEventsAsync() method contains the code that will take each incoming alarm event and log it to SQL Database and create a push notification toast message to send to the alarms Notification Hub.

```
// get the alarm message from event hub
var stream = eventData.GetBodyStream();
var bytes = new byte[stream.Length];
stream.Read(bytes, 0, (int) stream.Length);
var json = bytes.Aggregate(string.Empty, (current, t) => current + ((char)
t).ToString());
var alarm = ModelManager.JsonToModel<BiometricReading>(json);


// lookup the user that raised the alarm
var user = _profile.GetById(alarm.participantid);

// log the alarm to biometrics database using the API
Rest.Post(new Uri(_biometricsApi), json);

//format the toast message
var biometric = string.Empty;
switch (alarm.type)
{
    case BiometricType.Glucose:
        biometric = "Glucose";
        break;
    case BiometricType.Heartrate:
        biometric = "Heartrate";
        break;
    case BiometricType.Temperature:
        biometric = "Tempurature";
        break;
    case BiometricType.Bloodoxygen:
        biometric = "Blood Oxygen";
        break;
    default:
        biometric = "Not Set";
        break;
}

// format the toast message
var toast = "<toast><visual><binding template = 'ToastText04'> " +
  $"<text id = '1'>{"Home Biomedical Alert"}</text>" +
  $"<text id = '2'>{"The " + biometric + " reading for " +
  user.firstname + " " + user.lastname + " is out of
  range."}</text>" +
  $"<text id = '3' >{"Contact: " + user.social.phone}</text>" +
  "</binding ></visual></toast>";

// forward the toast to Notification Hub for push
hub.SendWindowsNativeNotificationAsync(toast).Wait();
```

In order to test the Reference Implementation real-time notification mechanism, you will need a mobile application that is associated with the Windows, Apple, or Google stores and is configured to receive notifications. The association is required so that you can retrieve the Package SID and Client Secret necessary to register the application with Notification Hub.

If you have a Windows Store account, you can create an application by reserving a name and then retrieving the Package SID and Client secret. To retrieve these values, reserve an application name, and then under the Services menu on the left, click Push Notifications. On the page, look for the Live Services site link and click through (see Figure 7-20).

Figure 7-20. *Windows Store Push Notification Instructions*

You will arrive on the page that provides the Package SID and Client Secret. Retrieve these values and enter them on the Notification Hub Configuration page (see Figure 7-21).

157

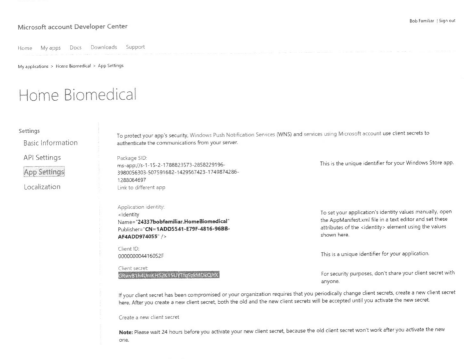

Figure 7-21. *Package SID and Client Secret*

The next step is to associate your Windows Store app with this reserved name in the Store. In Visual Studio, select Project ➤ Store ➤ Associate App with Store. You will be promoted to log into your store account, and you will receive a list of your reserved names. Select the one that you just created and move through the wizard (see Figure 7-22).

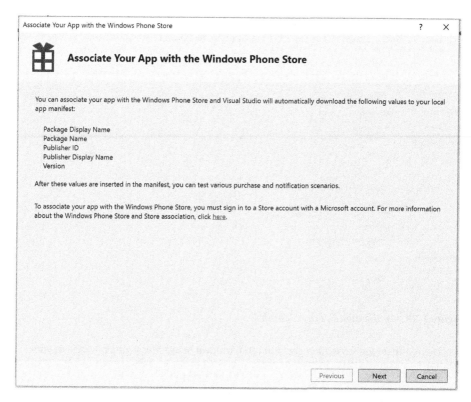

Figure 7-22. Windows Store Association Wizard

Open the Package Manifest, and on the Application Tab, set the Toast Capable option to 'Yes' (see Figure 7-23).

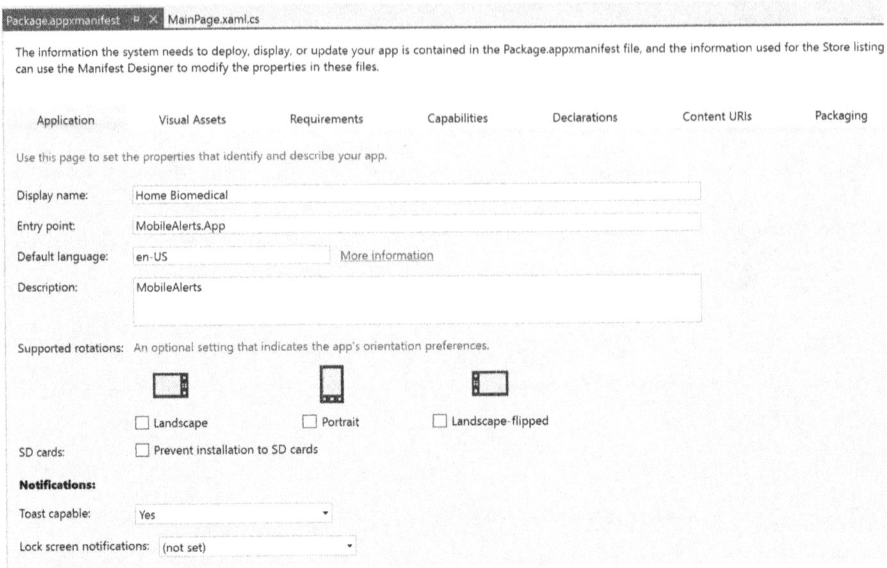

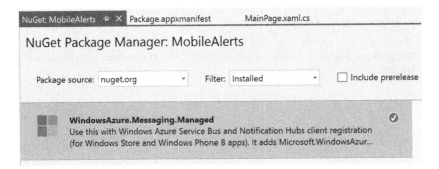

Figure 7-23. *Application Package Manifest*

Using NuGet Package Manager, add the Windows Azure Messaging package to your solution (see Figure 7-24).

Figure 7-24. *Windows Azure Messaging Package for Notification Hub Clients*

At application startup, create the hub client and the channel on which the push notifications will arrive. This creates a registration between the client application and the alarms push notification endpoint.

```
hub = new NotificationHub("alarms", "<notificaiton hub connection tring");

var channel = await PushNotificationChannelManager.
        CreatePushNotificationChannelForApplicationAsync();

await hub.RegisterNativeAsync(channel.Uri);
```

Testing Push Notifications

To test your mobile application, start the BioMax Simulator and then start your mobile application. You can optionally run the Biometrics Alarm Worker solution locally if you want to set breakpoints in that project. As alarms are picked up by the Stream Analytics jobs, they will be routed to the alarms Event Hub. There they will be picked up the Biometrics Alarm Worker who formats push notifications and sends them to the alarms Notification Hub. The Notification Hub will then push the notifications to any app that has an open channel on that hub. Figure 7-25 shows both the dashboard showing all biometric data being tracked in real time and the mobile app showing an alert toast.

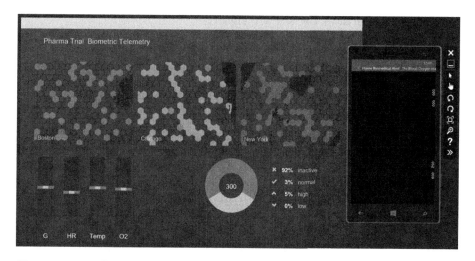

Figure 7-25. *Real-Time Dashboard and Mobile Alerts*

Real-Time Data Visualization

The biometrics-store Stream Analytics job routes device readings to SQL Database. Since the data is a bit cryptic, it makes sense to wrap the data with an API that provides context and, if necessary, business logic so that the data is provided in a meaningful way to the application.

There are many libraries, controls, and products that can be used to create data visualizations in responsive web applications. The Reference Implementation includes a sample application that uses AngularJS, Bootstrap, and D3 to create a wallboard-style dashboard that displays the device locations on maps of New York, Boston, and Chicago. It aggregates sensor reading data on gauges and provides examples of data aggregation (see Figure 7-19).

Biometrics API

The Biometrics API provides a contextual API for accessing the device readings stored in SQL Database. When used in conjunction with ASP.NET SignalR, the API can be used to provide real-time updates to client applications. SignalR allows bi-directional communication between server and client. Servers can push content to connected clients the instant it becomes available. SignalR supports Web Sockets, and falls back to other compatible techniques for older browsers.

■ **Note**　For more information on SignalR, including documentation and sample code, visit the official SignalR web site at `www.asp.net/signalr`.

Each row of data in the database contains a device id, participant id, the longitude and latitude coordinates for the location of the device, a time stamp, a sensor id, and a value. Since the data is flowing in real time, the API will return a specified number of rows of the most recent data. There are three endpoints:

```
// return the last N-number of readings by device id
biometrics/device/{deviceid}{/count/{count}

// return the last N-number of readings by participant id
biometrics/participant/{participantid}/count/{count}

// return the last N-number of readings by city and sensor
// type where sensor type is glucose, heartrate, temperature
// or bloodoxygen
biometrics/city/{city}/type/{type}/count/{count}
```

The Home Biomedical Reference implementation has pre-defined a set of 300 participants who are located in Boston, New York, and Chicago. These city names can be used as arguments to the Biometrics API along with the name of the sensor type and a count of records. For example, a possible invocation of the Biometrics API would be

```
http://biometricsapi.azurewebsites.net/biometrics/city/boston/type/glucose/
count/10
```

The data returned would be formatted as depicted in Figure 7-26.

```
▼<BiometricReading>
   <deviceid>f7e1f45d-9e4b-4d2d-ab3f-035928bbdc37</deviceid>
   <latitude>42.29652</latitude>
   <longitude>-71.138602</longitude>
   <participantid>59df0dae-8ff9-4652-9d02-f236f3b5bdcd</participantid>
   <reading>2015-07-15T20:57:07.68</reading>
   <type>Glucose</type>
   <value>184</value>
 </BiometricReading>
▼<BiometricReading>
   <deviceid>4b65017a-74fc-4bc2-8feb-65d9feb73c2c</deviceid>
   <latitude>42.258357</latitude>
   <longitude>-71.255878</longitude>
   <participantid>02a3d29f-c009-4176-8cce-03337abeb02d</participantid>
   <reading>2015-07-15T20:57:07.077</reading>
   <type>Glucose</type>
   <value>161</value>
 </BiometricReading>
▼<BiometricReading>
   <deviceid>3769ade1-06ce-41a0-808f-a1fe7c963f46</deviceid>
   <latitude>42.269741</latitude>
   <longitude>-71.09219</longitude>
```

Figure 7-26. *Biometrics API JSON*

■ **Note**   The Biometrics-related solutions can be found in Microservices\Biometrics.

Summary

IoT is not new. Devices connected on a network delivering real-time telemetry have been around for a long time. Think about the connectivity and telemetry acquisition that NASA put in place for the first trip to the moon in 1969. Mission control was monitoring every aspect of the hardware, the capsule, and landing module, as well as the biometrics of the astronauts through their suits.

What has changed in the past couple of years is the commoditization and proliferation of sensors and devices and the commoditization of the services necessary to connect to these devices and ingest the sensor data at volume. Azure is at the forefront of this movement, providing an IoT microservices stack that allows you to bring these types of solutions to market in days and weeks rather than months and years. Azure Event Hub, Stream Analytics, and Notification Hub provide the necessary foundational microservices that, when combined with your custom Microservices, deliver a highly scalable, fault tolerant, reliable Software as a Service IoT solution.

CHAPTER 8

■ ■ ■

Service Fabric

You now know that Azure *is* a platform built from the ground up using a microservice architecture. You have examined the evolution from monolithic architectures to microservices for modern cloud-native applications. You learned what a microservice is, and you looked at how Azure provides a rich set of managed services on which you can build Software as a Service solutions such as SQL Database, DocumentDb, Service Bus, and many more. You learned how Azure allows you to define application containers that provide elastic scale and fault tolerance, and are managed completely through automation. You learned about the very pattern that is at the heart of Azure and how to leverage that pattern to deliver modern software.

In the spring of 2015, at the annual //build conference, Microsoft announced Service Fabric. Service Fabric is the public release of the foundational services, runtime, and infrastructure that Microsoft uses to build, deploy, and manage their own first-class cloud services such as SQL Database, DocumentDb, Bing Cortana, Halo Online, Skype for Business, In Tune, Event Hubs, and many others.

This early preview release of Service Fabric is targeted at startups and ISVs that must provide the most scalable and fault tolerant solutions. It introduces some new terminology and concepts as well as programming models and related tools for building, deploying, and maintaining stateful and stateless microservices. This chapter will provide a primer on Service Fabric using the Developer Preview, and it provides an example using the RefM Microservice from the reference implementation.

Concepts

Service Fabric is a distributed systems platform that provides a rich set of built-in capabilities for creating scalable, available, consistent, reliable, and manageable solutions consisting of traditional monolithic applications or microservices. It solves some of the toughest problems that developers and operations face when supporting complex, mission-critical applications by providing platform services for hyper scale, partitioning, rolling upgrades and rollbacks, health monitoring, load balancing, replication, and failover. It allows you to focus on the design and implementation of the solution while Service Fabric provides the runtime management.

Service Fabric provides a model by which you package the code for a collection of related microservices and their configuration manifests into *Application Packages*. Application Packages are deployed and activated across Service Fabric *Clusters*.

Clusters are made up of a few to thousands of VMs. You can pack each VM in your cluster with many application package deployments. Using this approach you can maximize your investment in your cloud resources by increasing the service density (the number of instances of your microservices that can run concurrently). Service Fabric will be initially supported on Windows with Linux soon to follow. It can be deployed to Azure, to on-premises servers or virtual machines and can be hosted in third-party environments. (see Figure 8-1).

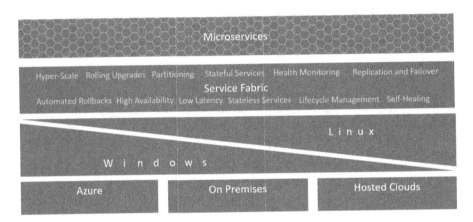

Figure 8-1. *Service Fabric Concepts*

Service Fabric defines two programming models, *Reliable Service* and *Reliable Actor*. Both Reliable Service and Reliable Actor give you the ability to create stateless and stateful microservices. Stateless microservices do not maintain state beyond individual request/response interactions and typically leverage message queues and in-memory caches to decrease latency and increase performance. Stateful microservices maintain state beyond the request/response interaction. They keep the logic and data close so that you can eliminate the need for queues and caches.

Platform Architecture

Service Fabric provides a comprehensive set of lifecycle management services that take care of cluster provisioning, package deployment, health monitoring, managing upgrades and rollbacks, and much more (see Figure 8-2).

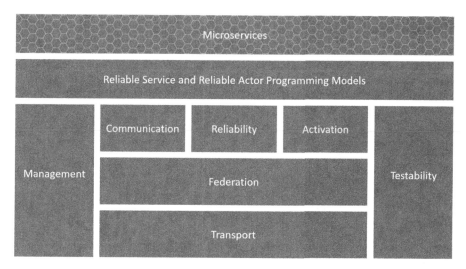

Figure 8-2. *Service Fabric Architecture*

- **Transport**: The Transport Service provides fast reliable messaging between all the Service Fabric service components.

- **Federation**: The Federation Service manages the coordination between nodes in a cluster. A cluster is a network-connected set of VMs or physical machines into which application packages are deployed. A node is an addressable unit in a cluster and have characteristics such as placement properties and unique IDs, and can join and leave clusters. The Federation Service can determine if a machine, VM, or service fails, and will provide automatic restart, reconfiguration, and redeployment capabilities.

- **Reliability:** The Reliability Service provides reliable replicated state storage, failover, and placement across cluster nodes for your microservices.

- **Activation**: The Activation Service gives you the ability to logically distribute your application packages across multiple nodes and partitions, and run multiple instances, different configurations, and different versions across your cluster environment.

- **Management**: The Management Service provides full lifecycle management capabilities covering provisioning, rolling upgrades, rollbacks, and monitoring.

- **Testability**: The Testability Service gives you the ability to inject actual failures in your run-time environment in order to test for various failure scenarios.

Application Model

An Application is a collection of Services which can be either traditional monolithic services or as we have been discussing throughout this book, microservices. When using Service Fabric along with microservices, each application does one thing and does it well and is defined by a collection of code, configuration, and data. Each service can be versioned and managed and upgraded independently (see Figure 8-3).

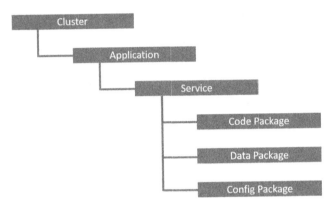

Figure 8-3. *Application Model*

A cluster consists of multiple nodes. Each node can host multiple application packages. Each application package is the lifecycle isolation unit and lifecycle management component for an application. An application is made up one of more services.

The details of what makes up an application are found in its application manifest, and a service is defined by its service manifest. A service consists of code, data, and a configuration package. As you have observed, a microservice can consist of several components such as a public API, a private API, a NoSql store, a console application, and so on. The ability to package together all the components that define a microservice and manage as a versioned deployment unit is a powerful construct and provides the isolation and deployment model required for a microservice architecture.

In Figure 8-4, the Service Fabric cluster is made up of six nodes running two application packages per node. The packages for Application Type A and Application Type B are distributed across the cluster, and there are two versions of each application running.

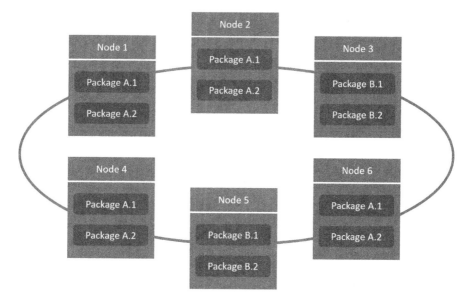

Figure 8-4. *Six-Node Service Fabric Cluster*

The act of distributing the application packages across the nodes and managing their lifecycle is handled by the Service Fabric runtime. If a service fails, it is restarted. If nodes fail, they are replaced, and the application packages are re-deployed and started.

Partitioning

Service Fabric supports both stateless and stateful service types. A stateless service type persists state to an external storage location such as SQL Database, DocumentDb or Service Bus Queues, Topics or Event Hubs. If a node on which an instance of this service is running goes down, another instance is automatically started on another node. Incoming requests are distributed across the stateless service endpoints.

A stateful service type maintains its own state and achieves reliability through replication between replicas on other nodes in the Service Fabric cluster. Stateful service types have a primary replica and multiple secondary replica instances. If a node on which a replica of a service is running goes down, a new replica is started on another node. If the replica happens to be the primary replica, a secondary replica is automatically promoted to be the new primary.

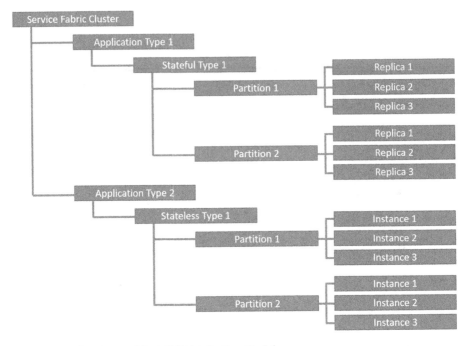

Figure 8-5. *Stateless and Stateful Distribution Model*

In addition to providing classic load balancing across service instances, Service Fabric provides a partitioning mechanism. Service instances can be divided into partitions which are then distributed across the Service Fabric cluster. There are three types of partitioning schemes:

- **Singleton**: The service is not partitioned.

- **Named**: Each service partition is given a unique name.

- **Ranged**: A number of partitions and an integer range defined by a low and high value are combined to distribute load. Each partition is responsible for a non-overlapping subrange.

For example, if you want to use a ranged partition schema with 5 replicas, 3 partitions, and a range of 00 to 99, you would define your ranged partitions as depicted in Figure 8-6.

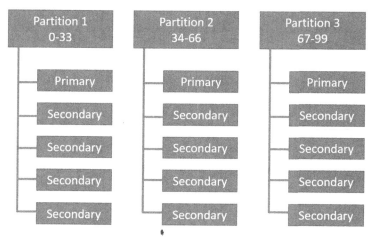

Figure 8-6. Ranged Partitioning Scheme

Programming Models

Service Fabric provides two APIs for building services: the Reliable Actors API and the Reliable Services API. Each programming model supports stateless and stateful services as well as the ability to plug in a communication protocol of your choice such as Web API, WCF, WebSockets, or TCP.

Reliable Service

Reliable Services can be used to create stateful services or used to create stateless services just like the microservices you have been using up to this point that use Web API as their communication protocol. Since you have done a good job of separation of concerns between the implementation of your services and the protocol layer, migrating to Service Fabric should not be difficult.

For stateful services, you use Reliable Dictionary or Reliable Queue classes to maintain state right within the code that implements your service. There is no need to employ an external store. This programming model is suitable for applications where you need to perform compute across multiple common units of state. A deployed instance of a stateful service is composed of a replica set. One of the replicas in the set is a primary, and the others are secondary. Read operations can be performed by both primaries and secondaries with the caveat that secondary reads may not be fully consistent. Write operations can only be performed on the primary and are automatically replicated to secondary replicas. A write quorum is achieved when a majority of replicas have acknowledged the write operations (see Figure 8-7).

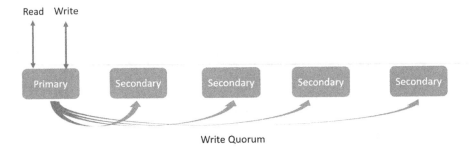

Figure 8-7. Stateful Reliable Service Write Quorum

Reliable Actor

A service based on the Reliable Actor programming model uses the actor pattern. The actor pattern defines an actor as an isolated unit of logic and state that communicates through asynchronous messaging. In Service Fabric, actors are isolated, single-threaded objects that encapsulate logic and state, and implement an interface of asynchronous methods that are used for passing messages between the other components of the system. This pattern is suitable for applications that require multiple independent units of state. A multi-player game is an example of an application that might use this approach. Each player can be represented by an actor that is managing their state within the game as well as the code that represents the AI for a player.

Service Fabric actors are virtual. They are not explicitly created or destroyed. When a request for an actor arrives, an actor is created. That instance will remain around and if not used for some period of time will get garbage collected. The value of data members of stateful actors is maintained on disk and replicated across multiple nodes in the cluster. That actor's state will be brought back into memory when that actor is reanimated. The data members of a stateless actor are not preserved. Service Fabric will distribute actors throughout a cluster and automatically migrate them to a new node if the node they are running on fails.

Service Fabric Example: Stateless Web API - RefM

To demonstrate how to create a stateless Reliable Service, let's migrate the existing RefM Public API to Service Fabric. Before we dive into the details on migrating existing Web API applications to Service Fabric, let's cover some background first.

Getting Started

At the time of this writing, Azure Service Fabric is available as a developer preview that you can download and work with in your local environment.

> ■ **Note**   Download the Service Fabric Developer Preview from
> http://azure.microsoft.com/en-us/updates/developer-preview-service-fabric/.

The preview consists of the SDK, a collection of samples, and several online articles that provide instructions and sample code. Follow the instructions to install the SDK and set up a local Service Fabric cluster that will be used as the deployment environment for the sample projects. You can download the Service Fabric samples from GitHub.

> ■ **Note**   Download the Service Fabric samples from GitHub at
> https://github.com/Azure/servicefabric-samples.

The Service Fabric SDK installs four project templates: a stateless and stateful template for the Reliable Service programming model and a stateless and stateful template for the Reliable Actor programming model (see Figure 8-8).

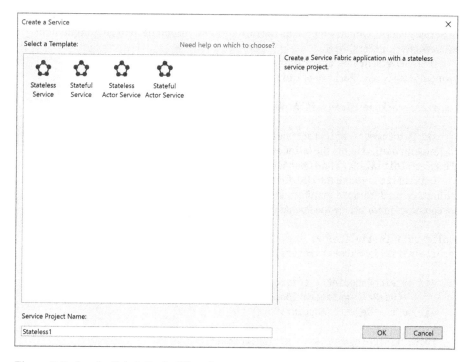

Figure 8-8. *Service Fabric Project Templates*

You can start with these templates or leverage the Service Fabric samples to jumpstart your experimentation with the SDK. Another good starting point for this application type is the web application sample included with the sample code you downloaded from GitHub. You can also follow along using the article referenced below to create a Reliable Service Web API.

■ **Note**   You will find a useful article on Web API Reliable Service at
http://bit.ly/1UMdKIf.

For this examination of Service Fabric, you will reference the ServiceFabricWebAPI solution located in the folder ServiceFabric\API folder in the supplied Git Repo.

Service Fabric Hosting Model

Since Service Fabric does not leverage IIS to host Web API, you will leverage the Katana implementation of the Open Web Interface for .NET (OWIN). OWIN allows you to write a web application that is decoupled from the host process, in essence creating a web server and placing that web server within the context of a host process. This is a perfect model for Service Fabric, which will provide the host process. All you need to do is implement the web server. Enter OWIN.

To use OWIN in your applications, reference the Microsoft.AspNet.WebApi. OwinSelfHost NuGet Package or run the following command in the NuGet Console:

```
> Install-Package Microsoft.AspNet.WebApi.OwinSelfHost
```

The OwinCommunicationListener class implements the OWIN contract. You can find the implementation in the file OwinCommunicationListener.cs. There are two methods of interest: Initialize() and OpenAsync().

Initialize is where the URL for the service is configured. The Service Endpoint settings are read from the manifest, and the listening address and publish address strings are constructed for use by the OpenAsync method.

```
public void Initialize(ServiceInitializationParameters
serviceInitializationParameters)
{
    var serviceEndpoint = serviceInitializationParameters.
        CodePackageActivationContext.GetEndpoint( "ServiceEndpoint");
    var port = serviceEndpoint.Port;

    this._listeningAddress = string.Format(
        CultureInfo.InvariantCulture,
        "http://+:{0}/{1}",
        port,
        string.IsNullOrWhiteSpace(this._appRoot) ?
            string.Empty: this._appRoot.TrimEnd('/') + '/');
```

```
        this._publishAddress = this._listeningAddress.Replace( "+",
            FabricRuntime.GetNodeContext().IPAddressOrFQDN);
}
```

The OpenAsync() method uses the listening and publish strings to start the web server. The OwinCommunicationListener class also provides methods for stopping the web server either through graceful means or due to an error.

```
public Task<string> OpenAsync(CancellationToken cancellationToken)
{
    ServiceEventSource.Current.Message( "Opening on {0}", this._publishAddress);

    try
    {
        ServiceEventSource.Current.Message( "Starting web server on {0}",
                this._listeningAddress);

        this._serverHandle = WebApp.Start(this._listeningAddress, appBuilder =>
                this._startup.Configuration(appBuilder));

        return Task.FromResult(this._publishAddress);
    }
    catch (Exception ex)
    {
        Trace.WriteLine(ex);
        this.StopWebServer();
        throw;
    }
}
```

The host process for a Service Fabric application is a console application. The implementation of this console application can be found in Program.cs. The Service Fabric Runtime object is used to register the StatelessWebAPI Service Type, which creates an instance of the StatelessWebAPI class.

```
public class Program
{
    public static void Main(string[] args)
    {
        try
        {
            using (var fabricRuntime = FabricRuntime.Create())
            {
                fabricRuntime.RegisterServiceType( StatelessWebAPI.
                ServiceTypeName, typeof(StatelessWebAPI));
                Thread.Sleep(Timeout.Infinite);
            }
        }
        catch (Exception e)
        {
            ServiceEventSource.
              Current.
                ServiceHostInitializationFailed(e);
            throw;
        }
    }
}
```

The StatelessWebAPI class creates the OwinCommunicationListener, passing in the root name of the application. The web server is created and runs within the host process, in this case a console app managed by Service Fabric.

```
using Microsoft.ServiceFabric.Services;

namespace StatelessWebAPI
{
    public class StatelessWebAPI : StatelessService
    {
        public const string ServiceTypeName = "StatelessWebAPIType";

        protected override ICommunicationListener
        CreateCommunicationListener()
        {
            return new OwinCommunicationListener("refm", new Startup());
        }
    }
}
```

Implement RefM Public Web API

By default, the application will run on port 80. Each service fabric solution will need to have a unique port number so you will want to get into the habit of modifying the port setting. The port setting is in the ServiceManifest file. Look for the <Endpoint> element and modify the Port attribute.

```
<Resources>
    <Endpoints>
      <Endpoint Name="ServiceEndpoint" Type="Input" Protocol="http" Port="8081" />
    </Endpoints>
  </Resources>
```

Modify the DefaultController to provide a status message when the root URL is invoked. This function could be enhanced to provide a more compelling user experience. For now, you simply want to know that the service is up and running.

```
using System.Web.Http;

namespace StatelessWebAPI.Controllers
{
    public class DefaultController : ApiController
    {
        [HttpGet]
        public HttpResponseMessage Index()
        {
            var message = new HttpResponseMessage
            {
                StatusCode = HttpStatusCode.OK, Content = new StringContent(
                    "RefM Reliable Service Available")
            };
            return message;
        }
    }
}
```

Add a reference to the RefPublicAPI NuGet package and an additional controller class called RefMController to the project. This class will provide the implementation of the RefM routes. Add your DocumentDb and Redis Cache connection strings in the constructor.

```
using System.Collections.Generic;
using System.Configuration;
using System.Web.Http;
using LooksFamiliar.Microservices.Ref.Models;
using LooksFamiliar.Microservices.Ref.Public.Service;
```

```csharp
namespace StatelessWebAPI.Controllers
{
    public class RefMController : ApiController
    {
        private readonly RefM _refM;

        public RefMController()
        {
            var docdburi = "[your-docdb-uri]";
            var docdbkey = "[your-docdb-key]";
            var redisuri = "[your-redis-uri]";

            _refM = new RefM(docdburi, docdbkey, redisuri);
        }

        [HttpGet]
        public List<Entity> GetAllByDomain(string domain)
        {
            return _refM.GetAllByDomain(domain);
        }

        [HttpGet]
        public Entity GetByCode(string code)
        {
            return _refM.GetByCode(code);
        }

        [HttpGet]
        public List<Entity> GetByCodeValue(string codevalue)
        {
            return _refM.GetByCodeValue(codevalue);
        }

        [HttpGet]
        public List<Entity> GetAllByLink(string link)
        {
            return _refM.GetAllByLink(link);
        }
    }
}
```

This controller is identical to the original RefM controller except that the routes are no longer defined using the Route Attribute but instead are defined at startup in the RouteConfig class located in the App_Start folder.

```
using System.Web.Http;

namespace StatelessWebAPI.App_Start
{
    public static class RouteConfig
    {
        public static void RegisterRoutes(HttpRouteCollection routes)
        {
            routes.MapHttpRoute(
                name: "Default",
                routeTemplate: "{action}",
                defaults: new { controller = "Default", action = "Index" },
                constraints: new { }
                );

            routes.MapHttpRoute(
                name: "GetAllByDomain",
                routeTemplate: "entities/domain/{domain}",
                defaults: new { controller = "RefM", action = "GetAllByDomain" },
                constraints: new { }
                );

            routes.MapHttpRoute(
                name: "GetByCode",
                routeTemplate: "entities/code/{code}",
                defaults: new { controller = "RefM", action = "GetByCode" },
                constraints: new { }
                );

            routes.MapHttpRoute(
                name: "GetByCodeValue",
                routeTemplate: "entities/codevalue/{codevalue}",
                defaults: new { controller = "RefM", action = "GetByCodeValue" },
                constraints: new { }
                );

            routes.MapHttpRoute(
                name: "GetAllByLink",
                routeTemplate: "entities/link/{link}",
                defaults: new { controller = "RefM", action = "GetAllByLink" },
                constraints: new { }
                );
        }
    }
}
```

To complete the RefM migration, specify the name 'refm' as the application name in the OwinCommunicationListener constructor call in StatelessWebAPI.cs.

```
using Microsoft.ServiceFabric.Services;

namespace StatelessWebAPI
{
    public class StatelessWebAPI : StatelessService
    {
        public const string ServiceTypeName = "StatelessWebAPIType";

        protected override ICommunicationListener CreateCommunicationListener()
        {
            return new OwinCommunicationListener("refm", new Startup());
        }
    }
}
```

Testing the Service

Once the service is running, use a browser to enter a RefM route such as http://localhost:8081/refm/entities/domain/LanguageCodes. This call will return the list of language codes from the reference store (see Figure 8-9).

Figure 8-9. *RefM Reliable Service*

The Service Fabric Visual Studio templates provide the PowerShell scripts to provision and deploy the application package to your local Service Fabric cluster. Once deployed, you can use the Service Fabric Explorer to view the details of the deployment (see Figure 8-10).

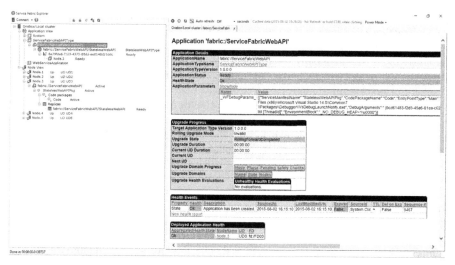

Figure 8-10. *Service Fabric Explorer*

The current Developer Preview version of Service Fabric only runs locally on your machine. While working with Service Fabric, I have found that F5 build and deploy from Visual Studio will not work past the first time due to an Access Denied error from Service Fabric. This happens because the application is still running even though you have stopped the debugger. It is necessary to remove the application from Service Fabric before each deployment. There are two PowerShell cmdlets that provide this ability.

```
> Connect-ServiceFabricCluster
> Remove-ServiceFabricApplication -ApplicationName 'fabric:/
ServiceFabricWebAPI'
```

The `Connect-ServiceFabricCluster` cmdlet will make sure you are talking to your local cluster environment. Since it is the only Service Fabric environment, this cmdlet does not require any parameters. The `Remove-ServiceFabricApplication` cmdlet takes a single parameter, the `'fabric:/'` based name of the application. This command will prompt you to confirm removal unless you add the `-Force` parameter. I have added a `Remove-FabricApplication.ps1` script to the solution for convenience.

Summary

Service Fabric represents a future state for microservice-based solutions running in Azure. It is Microsoft's next generation platform for creating cloud-native, highly scalable, fault tolerant, resilient, autonomous, and automated microservices. Service Fabric provides a rich set of deployment, management, and monitoring capabilities that make moving to microservice architecture more straightforward than ever before.

As demonstrated, it is not difficult to migrate existing Web API solutions to Service Fabric. This has powerful ramifications. The investments you make today in microservice architecture, adopting Azure Services and creating your own cloud services and web APIs are long-term investments that will continue to pay dividends as the Azure platform evolves. You will be optimizing your solutions to take full advantage of the platform.

Taking those first steps in this direction can be the most difficult part of the process. You must as a team commit to a DevOps culture as well as lean engineering and Agile principles along with a modern development process that emphasizes customer satisfaction through frequent delivery of working code. You must rethink your monolithic designs and look for opportunities to carve off capabilities and reimagine your solutions by leveraging microservice architecture, Azure Services, and of course automation.

My goal in writing this book was to provide you with a new perspective on application architecture and cloud platforms and afford you the opportunity to consider how you are developing software today, to re-imagine your solutions as fully automated, cloud-native services and consider how you might get started adopting this approach. You have learned that Azure is a platform built form the ground up using a microservice architecture and that it provides you the best opportunity to realize a fully automated software solution that delivers a high-value experience for your customers and a high-velocity platform that drives business impact. As Azure is an ever evolving platform, I do expect that the contents of this book will evolve as well. I look forward to interactions online and in person with you, the reader, as we take this journey together into the deep blue. Code on!

Index

Get the eBook for only $5!

Why limit yourself?

Now you can take the weightless companion with you wherever you go and access your content on your PC, phone, tablet, or reader.

Since you've purchased this print book, we're happy to offer you the eBook in all 3 formats for just $5.

Convenient and fully searchable, the PDF version enables you to easily find and copy code—or perform examples by quickly toggling between instructions and applications. The MOBI format is ideal for your Kindle, while the ePUB can be utilized on a variety of mobile devices.

To learn more, go to www.apress.com/companion or contact support@apress.com.

Printed in the United States
By Bookmasters